THE CENTERS OF CIVILIZATION SERIES

SARDIS
in the Age of Croesus

SARDIS
IN THE AGE OF CROESUS

By John Griffiths Pedley

UNIVERSITY OF OKLAHOMA PRESS : NORMAN

The paper on which this book is printed bears the water-mark of the University of Oklahoma Press and has an effective life of at least three hundred years.

Library of Congress Catalog Card Number: 67-64447

Copyright 1968 by the University of Oklahoma Press, Publishing Division of the University. Composed and printed at Norman, Oklahoma, U.S.A., by the University of Oklahoma Press. First edition.

Sardianis

Preface

◆

THIS BOOK is intended for anyone who might chance to be interested in the cultural and historical events which surrounded the familiar and legendary Croesus. Although it is directed principally at the intelligent layman, I hope it may also provide amusement and some degree of stimulus for the more scholarly world. In accordance with the aims of the Centers of Civilization Series, I have tried to focus more on manifestations of Lydian culture than on political history. Thus, aesthetic developments in architecture, sculpture, and painting and the daily life of the citizens of Sardis have received as much attention as political and military events. Similarly, conforming with the plan of the series, the book has been written directly from the ancient sources and from the archaeology. In certain aspects the archaeological evidence has proved of paramount importance, and the book could not have been written without the material provided by the recent and continuing Harvard-Cornell excavations.

My own interest in Sardis, and particularly in Sardis of the Mermnad period (*ca.*650–*ca.*550 B.C.), was spurred by an invitation to participate in the excavations in the summers of 1962, 1963, and 1964. Subsequently, my doctoral dissertation for Harvard University was written under the title, "Studies in the History and Archaeology of Sardis"; those essays provide the groundwork, in rather more scholarly form, for the present volume.

The books and articles listed in the Selected Bibliography give some indication of the extent of my debt to the work of other scholars. In quoting from ancient texts, I have, for the most part, relied on existing translations. Occasionally, minor alterations have been made. The quotation from Alcman at the beginning of the Prologue is taken from J. M. Edmonds' version (The Loeb Classical Library) with minor modifications; the passage from Tacitus appears in the Modern Library edition in a translation by A. J. Church and W. J. Broadribb; and Whiston's version of Josephus (Bohn's Standard Library) is the one used here. The passages from Homer are borrowed from Richmond Lattimore's translation (The University of Chicago Press), and the quotation from Virgil in Chapter II is reproduced from the translation of F. O. Copley (The Bobbs-Merrill Company, Inc.). The translation of Herodotus which appears at the head of Chapter III is that of J. E. Powell (Oxford, Clarendon Press); the version of Bacchylides at the head of Chapter V is taken from Arthur S. Way's translation in Oates and Murphy, *Greek Literature in Translation*; the excerpt from Xenophon at the head of Chapter VI, is reproduced from the translation by Walter Miller (The Loeb Classical Library). The use of all these translations is gratefully acknowledged. The two plans are taken from the archives of the current Sardis Exploration by kind permission of the field director, Professor G. M. A. Hanfmann. The maps were drawn by H. F. Keuper of the Department of Geography of the University of Michigan: they are based on Kiepert's and preserve his spelling of place names.

I am indebted most of all to Professor Hanfmann—for the privilege of excavating for him at Sardis, for permission to publish evidence gathered in the new excavations and for giving most generously of his time to read the manuscript of this book and suggest many important improvements. I cannot thank him enough. I hope this volume may serve to intensify interest in Sardis, and allow its readers to share the excitement I have felt thinking about a man whose brightness and boldness staggered the world many years ago.

JOHN GRIFFITHS PEDLEY

Ann Arbor, Michigan
October, 1967

Contents

◆

SARDIS
in the Age of Croesus

Prologue: The Historical City

◆

No oaf nor lout are you,
but a man of highest Sardis.—ALCMAN.

ARISTOTLE believed that man was born to live in cities.
Only in an urban environment could he readily grow to
reach his highest state of development, not only politically,
but also intellectually, socially, and spiritually. This growth
was occasioned in antiquity by the association of the citizens, by their interacting one against another, and by their
conversation, their argument, and their curiosity; and it
was in the capital cities, the centers of civilization, that
intellectual ferment was most likely to beget spiritual satisfaction. This potential for growth and satisfaction for the
individual citizen is one of the characteristic qualities of the
ancient city, which the leading communities shared. Yet,
as each partook of this generalized and shared quality, each
also had its own uniquenesses, its own fames, and its own
traditions and glories, and the loyalty of the individual
citizen was as much to his city as to his country.

Such a city was Sardis, situated in what today is Turkey
some sixty-five miles inland from twentieth-century Izmir
and the Aegean coast. In antiquity she was the capital city
of the kings of Lydia. She was a city characterized in a
physical sense, according to the fifth-century Greek historian Herodotus, by houses built of reeds or mud brick
and roofed with thatch. This domestic architectural fact
provides one of the less dramatic peculiarities of ancient

3

Sardis. In spite of this, she was a city of which her citizens could be justly proud, and from which reflected glory shone. "No boor are you nor peasant but a man of highest Sardis," exclaimed the poet Alcman, self-exiled in Doric Sparta and writing towards the end of the seventh century B.C.

Around the then-known world the news of Sardis' distinction rang, from Persia to mainland Greece, from Egypt to the northern wastes, and for some one hundred years spanning the period from about 650 to 550 B.C., she was the acknowledged capital of one of the most powerful, richly endowed, and expressive countries of the world. This is the period of the Mermnad Dynasty, whose first king was Gyges and whose last the legendary Croesus, and it is to this century of growth, flourishing, and sudden extinction that our interest shall principally be directed. To be a citizen of Sardis at that time was to be a citizen of the most sophisticated country in the world, where Lydian art and architecture and the Lydian *modus vivendi* shone briefly like a meteor in the sky of the Greek awakening.

Another dynasty preceded the Mermnads in control of Sardis, a dynasty called by Herodotus the Heraclids, whose ancestry was traced from Heracles, and whose first king in Sardis was Agron and whose last the ill-fated and uxorious Candaules, whom the Greeks called Myrsilus. Herodotus even records the names of those who ruled over Lydia before Agron and says that they were descendants of Lydus, son of Atys, from whom the whole people received its name. The Sardian Heraclids were descended from Heracles in quite regular manner: Heracles' involvement with a female slave of Iardanus resulted in the appearance of Alcaeus, whence, a generation at a time, came Belus, Ninus, and Agron, the first to rule in Sardis. The Heraclid control of Sardis lasted in uninterrupted progression for twenty-two generations, a period, according to Herodotus, of no less than 505 years, until its termination at the hands of Gyges, son of Dascylus, of the family of the Mermnads. Herodotus calculated that Agron, the first of the Heraclids in Sardis, took the city somewhere around 1200 B.C.

The archaeology records that a great conflagration swept Sardis and destroyed the city at the end of the Bronze Age. Whether the Heraclids were responsible for the devastation or moved into and took over a decapitated society in Sardis, the destruction of the city and the Heraclid assumption of power seem necessarily related. Thereafter, as the archaeology tells us, the Mycenaean Greeks penetrated as far inland into Anatolia as Sardis. Quantities of pottery of the types known as Late Helladic IIIC (*ca.* 1200 B.C.–*ca.* 1050 B.C.) and Protogeometric (*ca.* 1050 B.C.–*ca.* 900 B.C.) found in Sardis speak eloquently of commercial contacts between Sardis on the one hand and the late Mycenaeans and the burgeoning Ionic-speaking Greeks of the Aegean coast on the other. It is from these Greeks that the people of Sardis were first to learn pictorial and decorative expression. Gyges the Mermnad put an end to the Heraclid supremacy about 680 B.C. A scant four generations later, Cyrus the Persian killed Croesus, the last Mermnad king, and Sardis fell into the hands of the Persians.

Subsequent to the overthrow of Croesus by Cyrus, Sardis retained her political significance, remaining the chief city of the area and the seat of the Persian satrap. As such, the city served not only as an administrative center but also as a Persian listening post, extending her antennae westward to receive impulses and suggestions of political movements from the Greek cities of the west. Politically she was a proto-East Berlin.

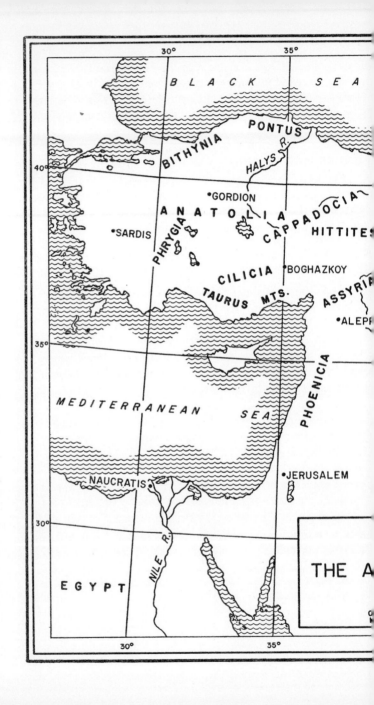

THE A

1. The ancient Near East

The Persians had reduced the Ionian cities of the coast, but in 499 B.C. these cities rose in revolt, aided and abetted by the Athenians and Eretrians with twenty-five ships from mainland Greece. In a spirited maneuver, recorded both by Herodotus and Charon of Lampsacus, another fifth-century Greek historian, the Ionian Greeks and their allies marched up the valley of the river Cayster, south of the valley of the river Hermus, in which Sardis is located, and, crossing the mountain ridge called Tmolus at dead of night, fell upon Sardis unexpected. Sardis was burned, and among the buildings destroyed was a temple of Cybele; it was the burning of this temple which the Persians were to cite as their excuse for the willful destruction of the temples of Greece some twenty years later.

But the revolt was not long-lived, and when the instigator of it all, Histiaeus, was taken prisoner, the Persian satrap in Sardis, Artaphernes, saw to it that no more trouble should come of him. In Sardis his body was impaled, and his head, embalmed, was sent to the Great King, Darius, in Susa. The Persians were vexed that their authority should be challenged, and, after again compelling the coastal cities to come to terms and reducing Miletus to ruins, launched a huge expedition against Greece herself. Turned back at Marathon in 490 B.C., they returned ten years later under their king, Xerxes: the Greek playwright Aeschylus enumerates for us the hordes of his army, among which citizens of Sardis served under their commanders Arcteus and Metrogathes. The Persians were beaten again, and Xerxes fled headlong from Athens to nurse his wounds in Sardis.

In the later part of the fifth century, the Persian satraps in Sardis busied themselves diplomatically in the great war fought between Athens and Sparta, restlessly attempting to seize some advantage. Tissaphernes imprisoned the great

Athenian general Alcibiades in Sardis, but he escaped; Cyrus the Younger met Lysander in Sardis and gave him money for the Spartans to assist their war effort. Sardis was very much a center of political and diplomatic activity. But Cyrus aimed at higher things for himself than provincial government and, raising the standard of revolt in Sardis, gathered together forces to oppose his brother, the king Artaxerxes. Xenophon, the Greek mercenary and historian, has written of the presence of ten thousand Greeks in Cyrus' army, summoned to Sardis, and of the great march from Sardis across Anatolia to defeat at Artaxerxes' hands at the battle of Cunaxa on the Euphrates in 401 B.C.

While politically Sardis remained an important focus, culturally she subsided and became a city where Persian manners mingled with the Lydian and where both were subject to the Greek expression more and more. We have only two examples of monumental architecture surviving from the Persian period in Sardis, and both show a marked movement away from the Greco-Lydian articulation of the late Mermnad era. The masonry of the so-called Pyramid Tomb, which may perhaps be identified with the grave of the Persian Abradatas, whom Xenophon records as being interred on a hill by the river Pactolus, is identical with that of one of the staircases (Staircase B) from the Persian palace at Pasargadae. Epigraphic evidence tells us that Lydian and Ionian masons were active in Susa in the time of Darius, and we might think that Cyrus copied Lydian masonry rather than understand that the influence moved from east to west. Yet the form of the Pyramid Tomb, with the stepped pedestal, owes its inspiration to Persian prototypes. The court of the Persian satraps in Sardis relied upon its own Persian architects, if not its own masons, and in the minor arts too its enthusiasm was more for jewelry in the court

9

style of Persepolis, and for expensive rugs and fancy clothes.

Most of our epigraphic evidence for the Lydian language comes from the Persian era (547–334 B.C.) and tells us that Persian was not adopted as the language of the common people, nor was Greek introduced as such. Only a single stone inscription in Greek survives from this period, and that but a single word. It is not until the end of the fourth century that Lydians began to use Greek with any fluency and to adopt Greek names for themselves. A recently discovered inscription from Ephesus, listing the names of some forty-five citizens of Sardis condemned to death for interfering with a religious procession sent from Ephesus to Sardis, demonstrates that at the time of the inscription (dated in the last quarter of the fourth century) a few of the citizens of Sardis had begun to assume Greek names, though the majority retained their Lydian appellations.

When Alexander the Great marched on Sardis, he encountered no opposition, and when he was still about ten miles away, the Persian satrap Mithrines met him with the chief burghers of the city, and the city with all its treasure was handed over. Alexander climbed the fortress acropolis of Sardis, saw with his own eyes the palace of the Lydian kings, and gave instructions for a temple to be built to Olympian Zeus. He used Sardis in exactly the same administrative way that the Persians had, as an important provincial capital. The governor lived in Sardis, and the city was garrisoned; it was here in 308 B.C. that Alexander's sister, Cleopatra, died.

It was in this period, that of Alexander and his successors (334–133 B.C.), that Sardis became a completely Greek city. At the beginning of the third century, Sardis was in the hands of Lysimachus, one of Alexander's generals, but Seleucus I, who had obtained the wealthy and important satrapy of Babylonia in the division of the provinces after Alexander's death and from whom the Seleucid Dynasty is named, captured the city from him in 282 B.C. For the Seleucids too Sardis was to be the capital of Asia Minor, and it was under their supervision that the total Hellenization of the city, with a constitution written along Greek lines, seems to have taken place in the last years of the third century. Recent epigraphic finds have proved that by this time none of the leading citizens used anything other than Greek names, though Lydian must have persisted among those less well off.

At about this time the great temple to Artemis and Zeus was dedicated. The monetary deposits in the base of the cult statue are evidence for such a date, and a surviving fragment of the colossal statue of Zeus bears a certain resemblance to the portraits of Achaeus, the usurper who controlled Sardis from about 220 to 215 B.C. Achaeus had been given full control of the trans-Tauric country by his cousin, Antiochus III (the Great), but power went to his head, and in 220 B.C. he made bold enough to declare himself king and to begin to strike coins in his own name. Seleucid Asia Minor became a separate kingdom briefly, for Antiochus III had first to deal with rebels closer to home. But in the summer of 216 B.C. he was able to turn west against Achaeus, and by 214 B.C. Achaeus was under heavy siege in Sardis. Polybius, the second-century Greek historian, records the siege of Sardis and the ruse whereby, after a full year, Lagoras the Cretan was instrumental in the capture of the lower town—the city was given over to fire and the sword. Achaeus withdrew to the citadel, whence he was lured by deceit, captured, and killed.

Epigraphic finds from the current excavations have shown that after the destruction of the city Antiochus showed great clemency to the Sardians, instructing his western regent, Zeuxis, to furnish financial assistance to the citizens in the reconstruction of their city. The city was rebuilt in Hellenistic plan. Polybius tells us that at the time of the siege Sardis already possessed a theater and a hippodrome, distinguishing characteristics of the Greek city, so by the turn of the century Sardis was fully Hellenized, linguistically, politically, and architecturally.

The Roman republic was now extending her sphere of influence eastward, and came face to face with Antiochus III at the great battle of Magnesia in 188 B.C. Defeated, Antiochus withdrew, and the Romans advanced up the valley of the Hermus to take possession of Sardis and her fortress, which they promptly handed over to their ally in Asia Minor, King Eumenes II of Pergamum. The Pergamene kings had long coveted Sardis, and there is some reason to suppose that Attalus I had briefly occupied the city during the years 228 to 220 B.C. before giving way to the vigorous advance of Achaeus. Now the city was theirs, but only briefly, for when the last Pergamene king, Attalus III, died in 133 B.C., he left his whole kingdom, and Sardis with it, to the Roman republic.

Attalus' will was ratified at Rome, and five commissioners were appointed to arrange the government of the newly acquired territories. In accordance with a clause of the king's will, the city of Pergamum was declared independent, and the only other city which seems to have been granted this privilege was Sardis. The future seemed bright, but already dark clouds were gathering in the north and east, and it was to be another fifty years before the Roman peace was securely established in western Asia Minor.

To the northeast of Sardis and Lydia, King Mithridates VI of Pontus was plotting the conquest of the whole of

Asia Minor. His own kingdom lay along the south coast of the Black Sea, but by about 110 B.C. he had extended his influence into southern Russia and had made the Greek cities of the Crimea tributary to him. By the turn of the century he had also extended his control southward and westward over the neighboring non-Roman states. By diplomacy, conquest, and intrigue in the years 100–90 B.C., Mithridates made himself master of the kingdoms of Cappadocia to the southeast and Bithynia to the west, so that he controlled all of Asia Minor north of the Taurus Mountains, with the single exception of the Roman province. To this his greedy eye turned.

Diplomatic negotiations between Rome and Pontus broke down in 89 B.C., and by the end of the year war was inevitable. The Roman armies were outnumbered and badly commanded. In a single campaign in 88 B.C., three Roman generals were defeated one by one, and Mithridates made his way victorious from Amaseia in Pontus to Ephesus on the Aegean coast. His route took him down the Maeander valley to the south of Sardis, and everywhere he showed leniency and generosity to the native Asiatic populations. It was not until he had reached Ephesus, however, that his commitment to a nationalistic and anti-Roman policy reached such proportions that he decreed the slaughter of all Romans and Italians resident in Asia. Some eighty thousand are said to have perished, and we may well believe that Roman blood in Sardis was shed freely. Plutarch, the Greek-born biographer and philosopher of the first century, identifies for us one of the Sardian victims of Mithridates' anger, naming him Alcaeus.

Disenchantment with their new self-styled liberator soon set in in the leading cities, and following the defeat of Mithridates' forces in mainland Greece and the capture of

Athens by the astute Roman general Sulla in 86 B.C., revolt broke out, first in Ephesus, then directly in Smyrna and Sardis. By the year 85 B.C., Mithridates' position had become untenable; terms were agreed upon between Sulla and him, and he withdrew dejected to Pontus. This was not the last that the Roman province was to see of him, but to all intents and purposes it was, and the Pax Romana descended on Asia Minor.

Under Roman rule Sardis continued to be an important and thriving center of trade, standing pointedly at the end of the old Persian royal road from Susa, down which caravans brought their merchandise from the east. Her powers and influence as the center of administrative government were, however, lost to Ephesus, and Ephesus and Smyrna became the leading cities of the Roman province. Yet Sardis was drawn into the commercial nexus of the Roman world, facing farther westward than she had ever done before, and in spite of the depredations of the taxgatherers in republican times, the city under Roman rule experienced great wealth and comfort. If her position as the most influential city politically and artistically in Asia had been lost with the death of Croesus, at this time she benefited greatly from her pivotal position as a trading center and from the cessation of military conflicts. Like all other cities of the Roman world, she reaped great rewards from the Roman inclination to law and order, straight roads, and the protection of capital.

Physically the city experienced her greatest period of expansion, most specifically in the second, third, and fourth centuries A.D. The Roman architects were especially enabled to impose Roman thought, in matters of planning and building, in those areas of the city devastated by the great earthquake of A.D. 17, recorded for us by the Roman historian Tacitus:

> That year twelve famous cities of Asia fell by earthquake in the night, so that the destruction was all the more unforeseen and fearful. Nor was there the means of escape usual in such disaster, by rushing out into the open country, for there people were swallowed up by the yawning earth. Vast mountains, it is said, collapsed, what had been level ground seemed to be raised aloft, and fires blazed amid the ruin. The calamity fell most fatally on the inhabitants of Sardis, and attracted them the largest share of sympathy. The emperor promised ten million sesterces, and remitted for five years all they paid to the exchequer or the emperor's purse.

Although Sardis had been the scene of the final conference between the adamant republican generals Brutus and Cassius before they marched north to their deaths at Philippi in 42 B.C., the city had been loyal to the emperors, demonstrating her fidelity to Augustus by conferring unusual honors on the young Gaius Caesar, the eldest son of Agrippa and Julia, whom Augustus had adopted. Sardis was rightly included in the generosity with which Tiberius assisted the suffering communities of Asia Minor after the earthquake.

Large Hellenistic buildings, such as the temple of Artemis and Zeus, were repaired and enlarged, and new buildings arose from the wreckage of the earthquake. There is much evidence in Sardis today of the building operations of the years following the destruction: Basilica C, the Odeion east of the theater, the theater itself, and, most conspicuously, the mighty Complex B, including a gymnasium, its vast marble forecourt, and the synagogue of Sardis. The gymnasium was built in the second century A.D., and in the early years of the third century the forecourt was added and the synagogue built.

The recent discovery of the synagogue, a large and imposing structure, confirms the presence of a large Jewish community in Sardis. The Jewish historian Josephus, writing in the first century A.D., reports that the Seleucid monarch Antiochus III had instructed Zeuxis, the governor of Lydia, to settle two thousand Jewish families, transported from Mesopotamia and Babylon, in the most important places of Lydia and Phrygia. Quite possibly some of these Jewish families were settled in Sardis. Surer evidence for the early (fifth century B.C.) presence of Jews in the city is found in the Bible: Obadiah, verse twenty, speaks of the captivity of Jerusalem which is in Sepharad. Most scholars now accept the identification of Sepharad as Sardis. A decree of Julius Caesar instructs the citizens of Sardis to allow the Jews to assemble and to have a place to hold their congregations, and continues:

> Let those that see to the provisions for the city, take care that such sorts of food as they shall esteem fit for their eating, may be introduced into the city.

This decree was passed by the senate and people in response to a delegation from Sardis of Jews who were Roman citizens, and indicates that forms of discrimination were being practiced against the Jews in Sardis at this time. In the time of Augustus too, the Jews of Asia Minor were persecuted by the Greek city administrations, and representations again were made to Rome. The Emperor himself wrote to the Roman proconsul, Caius Norbanus Flaccus, instructing him not to forbid the Jews to assemble, however many they were, and to allow them to send money to Jerusalem: Flaccus in turn wrote to the Sardians.

During the reign of Trajan (A.D. 98–117), feuds broke out

in Asia Minor between some of the cities, and even within the cities themselves, where civil discord bred wildly, inflamed by class hatred. Sardis was not exempt. Plutarch had written comfortingly in the first century to a citizen of Sardis driven into political exile, and Apollonius of Tyana wrote copiously to the citizens of Sardis begging them to desist from civil strife.

Cities vied with one another in the matter of rank and titles, so that by the time of the reign of Marcus Aurelius (A.D. 161–80), Sardis proclaimed herself "Metropolis of Asia and all Lydia," "Autochthonous," "Friend and Ally of Rome," and "Temple Warden of the Augusti." A newly found dedication to Caracalla (emperor A.D. 211–17) sees Sardis with daring imagination describing herself also as "Protochthonous," as well as "Temple Warden of the Augusti for the second time" and "Home of the Supreme Emperor." To this dazzling display of titles there was little that Elagabalus (emperor A.D. 218–22) could add beyond granting the city a third temple wardenship, a privilege revoked when he died, but restored by the emperor Gallienus (A.D. 260–68). (Originally reserved for cities responsible for temples dedicated to the worship of emperors, such as Smyrna, Pergamum, and Ephesus, "temple warden" was later given to other cities and used by them to bolster their claims. The extremes reached by such claims are indicated by the epithet "autochthonous" [native]; to improve on that, "protochthonous" was invented.)

Christianity was strong in the city by the second century, and Melito, bishop of Sardis, remonstrated to the emperor, Marcus Aurelius, about the treatment of Christians. The Revelation of St. John the Divine tells us that Sardis was one of the oldest Christian communities in Asia, yet at the time of the pagan revival and the apostasy of the emperor

Julian (A.D. 361–63), it was in Sardis that devotees of the old religion were found. Chrysanthius of Sardis was appointed high priest of the country, and derived support for his pagan views not only from his fellow Sardian, Eunapius, but also from the prefect of Asia, Justus, a more than enthusiastic pagan zealot.

To the early Byzantine period, or more specifically to the fifth to the early seventh centuries, can now be assigned the construction of the new defensive fortification wall. This wall encircled most of the city, though contemporary buildings have been found outside the wall, and these especially in the valley of the gold-bearing Pactolus River. The precise date of the construction of the fortification perimeter is not known, but the Gothic scare in A.D. 400, of which Zosimus, the fifth-century historian, tells us, may have provoked frenzied defensive activity. Somewhat later a large shopping complex was built, and the third-century marble court to the gymnasium was repaired. Close by, and immediately to the south of the road which superseded the thirty-foot-wide Roman road, itself the successor of the royal road which ran from Sardis to the Persian capital, the imposing residence of a dignitary of the church was constructed.

Yet Christianity in Sardis was not destined for longevity, and with the Sassanid-Byzantine struggle extending its tentacles of violence and ruin further and further, Sardis was embroiled. In the early seventh century, in the reign of the noble emperor Heraclius, the city was destroyed. The destruction was savage and brilliant, fire and sword were at play, and the responsibility in all probability lies at the feet of the Sassanid invaders in the years A.D. 616–17. Khosroes II had struck again and had put an end to the antiquity of Sardis. The city survived only as scattered hamlets and an acropolis until the conquest of Tamerlane in A.D. 1405 and her final extinction.

These in brief outline are the lives of the city of Sardis, leading her from the obscurity of the prehistoric period through the Mermnad heyday in the seventh and sixth centuries B.C. to the prosperity of the early Byzantine phase and her sudden death at the hands of Khosroes. Her span of life, historically documented, was a thousand years, her age of glory a single century, and it is to an examination of that century, and the contributions made in it by her kings and citizens in terms of social, cultural, and political development, that we now turn.

I

Sardis and Lydia

♦

Mesthles and Antiphos were leaders of the Maionians,
sons of Talaimenes, who was born of the lake Gygaian:
these led the Maionian men whose home was beneath Mount Tmolos.

*—*Homer.

THE CAPITAL CITY of the kings of Lydia was situated at the northern foot of the Tmolus range, nestling beneath the protection of a mountain chain that ran from the Aegean Sea to the foothills of the great upland Anatolian plateau. She lay some 100 kilometers up the valley of the loitering Hermus River from the Aegean, and 540 stades (67 miles; one stade equals one-eighth of a mile), or three days' journey, from Ephesus, as Herodotus and Xenophon would have us believe. Northward, eastward, and westward from the city and either side the east-west-flowing Hermus, stretched the plain of the valley, a plain known in antiquity as the Sardiane. Beyond the plain to the north was located the royal Lydian cemetery, now called the Bin Tepe, the Thousand Mounds. Yet farther to the north, beyond the mounds of the royal cemetery were the Gygaean Lake, the pass to Thyatira, and the river Hyllus, which flows south-westward to join the Hermus roughly midway between Sardis and the sea. Southward loomed the Tmolus.

Describing the Tmolus, Chishull, the learned and wandering English parson who visited Sardis in 1699, says it is "pleasant and garnished with an infinite variety of plants, shrubs and trees. Besides a fine prospect of the country, the traveller is amused with impending rocks, perpendicular precipices, and the murmurs of a brook, probably the Pactolus. On the top is a fruitful vale between two lofty ridges, with a vein of marble as clear and pellucid as alabaster."

To the west the Hermus wound his desultory way through fertile fields to the sea, following a course approximately parallel to that of his brother rivers, the Caicus to the north, the Cayster and the Maeander to the south. And to the east reared the burned lands, an old volcanic region described by the first-century geographer Strabo. These scorched lands covered five hundred stades in length and four hundred in width, the valleys were covered with ashes, and the rocks and hills were blackened as if by fire. The three principal volcanic craters were visible in Strabo's time, and a number of hillocks formed of lava also attested the igneous action which had taken place. Beyond the burned lands rose the high inland plateau.

Although Herodotus placed the boundary between Lydia and Phrygia, the kingdom which lies adjacent to Lydia to the east, at Carura, the extent of actively controlled Lydian territory is as uncertain as the location of Carura itself. Historians relate the presence of Lydians in the Troad, at Abydus and Dascylium, elsewhere at Magnesia and Colophon, and during the glorious days of the Mermnad Dynasty, all these places must have fallen within the orbit of Lydian influence. Inscriptions written in the Lydian language are predominantly from Sardis itself, and of the rest, most come from the Hermus Valley area from Manisa in the west to Emre in the east. However, inscriptions written in Lydian characters have been recovered from the valley of the Cayster too. If the boundaries of the Lydian empire cannot be identified with any great precision, at any rate the concentration of similarly constructed burial mounds and chambers in the Hermus Valley amply illustrates the whereabouts of the focus of Lydian power.

The acropolis of Sardis was perched defiantly on the northernmost spur of a north-south conglomerate ridge protruding from the flank of the Tmolus. Even its southerly face is steep and hard to climb. Alexander the Great himself scaled the acropolis and exclaimed at the strength and impregnability of the triple *enceinte* and at the natural setting. On either side of the acropolis, streams flow northward from the mountain range to meet the Hermus: the sands of the torrent Pactolus, rich with gold, were to make the city famous. Almost inaccessible, this vantage point may have been the magnet which drew the earliest settlers. It was easily defensible. The position strategically commanded the east-west route (later to become the Persian royal road) from the Anatolian highlands, Syria and Armenia, to the sea. Later a road ran northward to Thyatira and Pergamum, but southward, towards Ephesus and Mycale, Tmolus barred the way.

The natural resources were attractive, and far more so than the original settlers may have imagined. Water, wood, and clay were, and are, abundant. The Hermus with his tributaries was at hand. Rainfall was regular and enriching, the mountains were thickly wooded, providing timber for warmth and housing, and the clay beds were many and micaceous, yielding plentiful materials for mud bricks, as well as for pots. Rich today in tobacco, vegetables, fruit, vineyards, and cotton, the region must then, too, have appealed to an incipient agricultural community. The fact that the area was later able to support, one after the other, the royal city of the Lydian kings, the chief city of a Persian satrap and a Seleucid governor, and a large and splendid Roman city, argues a high early potential.

In historical times marble was found in the Tmolus, and Sardis was the place where, if we may believe Pliny the Elder, writing in the first century A.D., the stones known as sards, from which seals were cut, were first discovered. It was the discovery of gold in the Pactolus, however, which rocketed Sardis to an important position in the political balance of power in the one hundred years from 650 to 550 B.C. Sardis was famed for her blankets and carpets, so that the land must have provided ample grazing, then as now, for sheep and goats; and for the longer cropping bovids and horses too, fodder was available. The horses of Sardis were swift, sturdy, and plentiful, and the Lydian cavalry became the terror of the world. The area was so rich that Sardis became proverbial for her wealth and luxury, and famed for her music, food, and perfume.

These were the natural resources of the area to which the first Lydians came, establishing themselves at the foot of the acropolis of Sardis and sheltering beneath its gaze. The date of their arrival is unclear. Some say that the Lydians arrived in Asia Minor at roughly the same time as the Phrygians, that is to say, at the end of the late Bronze Age. Others suggest a linguistic relationship between the Lydian language and Hittite, the language of the great kings who inhabited and controlled the upland Anatolian plateau in the third and second millennia B.C., and propose accordingly that the Lydians may have arrived in western Asia Minor as early as the beginning of the second millennium B.C.

Nor do we have any clear knowledge of the limits of the earliest settlements and villages. Isolated soundings at Sardis have shown that the culture of the city at the end of the

Bronze Age seems to have been characteristically Anatolian: the late Bronze Age levels, reached only in one spot, have shown cremation burial and a shabby circular hut, constructed of branches and reeds and mud. Yet there were already contacts with Greece and the Mycenaean empire, enough perhaps to justify the existence in the literary record of legends which join Lydia with Greece. Annually there is increasing evidence of Mycenaean penetration of western Asia Minor, and sherds of the type classified as Late Helladic IIIC recovered from the lower levels at Sardis indicate cultural contacts between the two worlds at the end of the Bronze Age.

In common with many other sites of the eastern Mediterranean, Sardis was destroyed by a fierce and uncompromising foe at the end of the Bronze Age; but at a time of great population disturbances and political upset, it is difficult to assess the responsibility accurately. The Herodotean sons of Heracles may have been responsible, just as similar legend records the damaging activities of the Heraclids in Greece and elsewhere at this time. Some support is lent to this suggestion by the discovery in Sardis not only of Late Helladic IIIC pottery but also of Greek sherds of the chronologically subsequent style, the Protogeometric. This speaks forcefully enough for Greek influences at work in Sardis and for an episode of intensive relations between Sardis and Greece in the period 1200–900 B.C. It strengthens the case for a Greek destruction of Sardis, but does not prove it.

Evidence from the Hittite archives records that the mighty King Tudhaliyas IV (1250–20 B.C.) directed a series of reprisal attacks against a league of states called the confederacy of Assuwa, which had banded together to defy his authority. Hittite influence stretched, in this area, at least as far west as the rock carvings and inscriptions at

Karabel and on Mount Sipylus near Magnesia lead us to understand, and the geographic location of these rebellious states is linguistically asserted to have been along the coast of the Aegean Sea and somewhat inland. A tribe Asias existed at Sardis in historical times, and some say that the name of the entire continent of Asia is derived from a single portion of the city. Here was the political center of the confederacy of Assuwa. Tudhaliyas IV, then, is a good candidate for the role of the destroyer of Bronze Age Sardis. Another possibility might suggest that this was the activity of wandering freebooters, perhaps homeward bound after the Trojan War (about 1250 B.C.), or of shady chieftains like the enigmatic Mopsus, glimpsed so fleetingly in the Hittite archives of Boğhazköy, yet involved in the political maneuverings of the Hittite governor Maduwattas and the Achaean Atarisiyas somewhere along the Ionian coast.

Linguistic similarity between the name Maduw-attas and the names of historical Lydian kings, like Aly-attes, Sady-attes, and Ady-attes, has prompted the suggestions that the Maduw-attas of the late Bronze Age in western Asia Minor was a Lydian and that quite possibly the language spoken by the Lydians of historical times was also spoken in the late Bronze Age. Yet both the names Sardis and Lydia appear to have had precursors and to have been late-comers. Sardis and its acropolis were called Hyde, and as such Sardis appears in Homer. It is not until the middle of the seventh century that Archilochus, the Greek iambic poet and warrior from the island of Paros, talks of Sardis. But by the time of Mimnermus, the plaintive Smyrnaean elegist, Alcman, and Alcaeus, the lyric poet from Lesbos, who all wrote towards the end of the seventh century B.C., the name had been assimilated into the poetic vocabulary.

Homer does not talk of Lydia and Lydians but always of Maeonia and Maeonians, and Hipponax asserts that Candaules, the last king of the dynasty which preceded the Mermnads, has a Maeonian name. Ancient historians theorize that Lydia was named after Lydus, whose descendants were the pre-Heraclid rulers of Sardis; this term makes its earliest appearance in the middle of the seventh century in Assyrian archives, where mention is made of the *lud-di*. Perhaps the Heraclidae are to be equated with the Maeonians, and it may have been they who, as a ruling class of warriors, imposed their will and their names on the local peoples at the end of the Bronze Age, calling the city Hyde and the country Maeonia. Subsequently, with the expulsion in the seventh century of the last Heraclid king, Candaules, who bears a Maeonian name, and the assumption of power by the Mermnads, Sardis was called Sardis and Lydia, Lydia. The native elements were thus reasserted and in this way the similarity between the names of earlier rulers, like Maduw-attas, and the Mermnads, Aly-attes, Sady-attes, and Ady-attes may be explained.

Although linguists support the view that the historically known Lydian language is the same as, or a derivative of, the language spoken in Sardis in the late Bronze Age, yet the material is far from conclusive and does not permit any decision about the precise character of the people living in Lydia at this time. Our knowledge of the Lydian language is based on texts written in an alphabet similar to the Greek, but the body of material available is not large. Until recently less than sixty texts were known. Now it has become clear that individual characters in the Lydian script make their appearance on pottery not later than the middle of the seventh century, and by the sixth and fifth centuries, graffiti (incised scratchings, normally irregular) and *dipinti* (painted inscriptions, often uneven) are common enough.

It had been thought that the Lydian alphabet was fairly well recognized and established, until the sensational discovery on August 17, 1963, of a monumental inscription at Sardis, of which many of the signs are Lydian, but some not. This inscription, of some thirteen lines and one hundred characters, was discovered built into a pier of the synagogue of the Roman period, and the find-spot gives no indication of the date of the original monument. The contents of the inscription are quite obscure, and most experts now believe that the language is not Lydian, but a related one. Only a single word may perhaps be understood, the Lydian *sfenas*, meaning property, but even this requires a willing eye and a well-disposed interpretation. This staggering find simply suggests that there is a good deal still to be learned of the Lydian language and Lydian writing and that there may have been more than one language spoken in Sardis. The care exercised in the cutting of this inscription and the size of the monument itself bear eloquent witness to the wide use and importance of this other tongue, or Lydian variant, used in Sardis. It too may have Bronze Age forebears.

In the late Bronze Age, then, Sardis, as far as we know, was a village community whose architecture was wattle and daub huts, and where intramural cremation burial in pithoi, large clay storage vessels, was practiced. The presence of imported Mycenaean wares, and imitation of Mycenaean decorative motifs, proves early contact with the Greeks. Similarly, the Hittite rock carvings and pithos burial point to eastward contact with the rulers of the Anatolian plateau. The people were linguistically Indo-European, and the end of the Bronze Age settlement is marked by a fiery conflagration about 1200 B.C.

In the deep soundings undertaken at Sardis in recent seasons, perhaps the most startling historical fact to emerge has been the continuation of Greek sherds to the lowest levels, continuing even to a greater depth than that at which Lydian painted Geometric pottery has ceased to be represented. Plentiful sherds of the Late Helladic IIIC and Protogeometric styles indicate the overpowering visual and decorative impact that Greek pottery made on the local inhabitants. Eleventh- and tenth-century Sardians liked things Greek. Hence, it is clear that the formulation of the Lydian Geometric style of pottery is entirely due to Greek influence, and the principal characteristics of its decorative vocabulary are taken from the Greek Protogeometric style. Some elements, such as the black-on-red technique, could, however, have been borrowed from southwestern Asia Minor. Stratigraphic considerations suggest a date of about 900 B.C. for the introduction of this Lydian Geometric style of painted pottery. Presumably local Sardian potters, who had been exposed to Greek painted pottery from Mycenaean times on, were suddenly spurred to decorate their own pots.

The emergence of this Geometric style was a creative achievement of high importance for Iron Age Lydia, and is clear evidence of heightened cultural and artistic activity. At the same time as the painted pottery was introduced, the Anatolian monochrome gray wares continued, and we need not assume that any change in population is implied by the introduction of painted pottery; it is simply that the local potters and painters were becoming more aesthetically aware, either through their experience of the imported Greek mainland wares or through their visits to the Ionian cities and actual contacts with Greek potters and painters working there. This significant and constant import of

Greek Protogeometric and Geometric wares into Sardis has one interesting historical implication. At Gordium, capital of the neighboring kingdom of Phrygia, a gap in habitation had been postulated between the end of the Hittite empire and the definitively ascribable Phrygian levels, 1200–800 B.C. Now continuity of habitation has been proved by a stratification extending over a millennium, from about 1800 to about 800 B.C. Similarly, the continuation of the Greek pottery through stratified levels at Sardis shows that Sardis was occupied continually from the thirteenth to the seventh century B.C.

For plastic or glyptic and architectural expression in Iron Age Sardis we have little evidence. The common houses seem to have advanced beyond the wattle and daub of the Bronze Age to mud brick set around clay floors, with postholes indicating support for some form of, presumably, thatched roofing.

Before the Mermnads came to the throne of Sardis, the Heraclids ruled Lydia for twenty-two generations, or 505 years. Allotting 170 years for the empire of the Mermnads, Herodotus calculated that the Heraclids assumed control of Sardis about 1221 B.C. This is a date based on a typically Herodotean chronology, based on generation counting, and has no absolute validity. What is significant is the notice of a change of dynasty around 1200 B.C., a fact substantiated by the archaeological material. Our presently available knowledge of the history of the Heraclids in Sardis is scant and the sources not very reliable. Herodotus glides over the period swiftly, and we are left with whatever is preserved of Xanthus, the fifth-century Lydian historian, mainly in Nicolas of Damascus' Universal History, written in the first century. Xanthus' *Lydiaka* seems to have been a mélange of things topographical, anecdotal, geological, and etymological, with snatches of folklore and technical history here and there, but it is our only guideline.

According to Xanthus, who wrote in Greek, and to other traditions, Meles was an early king of Lydia, in whose reign a great famine swept the land, and the people in their superstition turned to augury. The gods instructed them to exact penalty for the violent death of the prince Dascylus, by whose demise Meles had profited. Meles was obliged to withdraw into voluntary exile to Babylon to expiate the murder. In the course of the divination, he invited the young Dascylus, son of the murdered Dascylus, whose mother had fled with him to Phrygia, to come to Sardis. As a diplomatic move this appears slightly banal, and the youth declined to leave the security of the Phrygian capital. So Meles was forced to leave. He handed over the kingdom to Sadyattes, from whom, incredibly enough, he received it back on his return from a three-year stint in Babylon.

Meles had an unusual concubine who presented him with a lion as an offspring. He did not immediately discard this cub, but, on the advice of the seers from Lycian Telmessus, he carried the cub around the walls of the citadel. In this way, the soothsayers had promised him, he would make the citadel impregnable. Unhappily, Meles neglected a single part of the wall, judging the ascent to that point to be too steep. This proved to be the very place at which, years later, in the time of Croesus, the Persians were able to enter the city.

Moxos the Lydian captured Atargatis, queen of Syria, and threw her with her son Ichthys into the lake of Ascalon where they were eaten up by fish. He was also responsible for driving Meles from the tyranny and for urging the

Lydians to offer tithes to the gods. The Lydians did so, but again a great famine struck them, and again they betook themselves to divination.

Two of these episodes concerning Meles are found in Xanthus' account and the third in Herodotus'. The stories are all sensational and anecdotal, and we should be cautious about placing any credence in them. They need not all refer to a single Meles, and Meles itself may have been a title rather than a personal name. Moreover, there are inherent historical improbabilities even in the episode which might contain narrative and actual facts. It is improbable that a tyrant, such as Meles appears to have been, would voluntarily go into exile, and even more improbable that he should be recalled. It is not perhaps irrelevant that what we have of the portions of Nicolas' Universal History concerned with Lydia and Sardis is preserved in two works compiled for Emperor Constantinus Porphyrygenitus in the tenth century A.D. and titled *Excerpta de Vitiis et Virtutibus* (Selections Concerning Vices and Virtues) and *Excerpta de Insidiis* (Selections About Ambushes). This material is almost by definition likely to be anecdotal.

Another early king of the Lydians, Adyattes, had twin sons, Cadys and Ardys, to whom he left his kingdom. Cadys, however, had an ambitious wife, Damonno, who took as her lover, Spermus, cousin of Cadys, and together they attempted to poison the husband. The draught prepared for them by a handy doctor was not strong enough to do away with Cadys, however, and the adulterous pair had to vent their frustration on the doctor himself, and wait for Cadys to die. This he did soon after. Thereupon Spermus and Damonno drove out Ardys and took posession of the kingdom.

Ardys made good his escape to Kyme, but Spermus hired

an assassin, Cerses, to remove Ardys, promising him his daughter in marriage as a reward. Cerses fell asleep, however, at a critical moment, and then by arrangement with Ardys, he returned to Sardis and beheaded Spermus. Nobody was saddened by this act, except presumably Damonno, since Spermus had a reputation among the Sardians for being a wicked fellow, and there had been another severe drought while he was king. He reigned for two years, but his name was not recorded in the king lists. Ardys was then recalled from Kyme by ambassadors from Sardis and restored to the kingship. He ruled best of all the Lydian kings excepting only Alcimius.

Here again the narrative is sensational and spicy, and fitted nicely into a collection of anecdotes entitled *de Insidiis* (About Ambushes). Further, the pith of the story concerns a prominent courtier, Spermus, and his taking the kingdom by taking the king's wife. This is an exact doublet of the Herodotean story of the first Mermnad king, Gyges, who took the kingdom by taking the wife of the last Heraclid king, Candaules. While it might be possible to suggest that these tales reflect the important position of the queen in the Lydian system, the story of Spermus and Damonno is a direct projection from Mermnad times into pre-Mermnad, and it is difficult to believe it as anything other than plain romance.

Other more improbable and anecdotal tales of the pre-Mermnad days abound. Cambles or Camblitas, a king of Lydia, was a hearty eater and drinker and such a glutton that one evening he butchered his wife and ate her; some said it was his greed, and others that he was bewitched by Iardanus. But in the morning, to his dismay, he found his wife's hand in his mouth and so he cut his own throat, since the awful deed had been divulged. This can surely be noth-

33

ing other than pure oriental fancy, but it gives us a good sense of the kind of sources on which Xanthus drew.

Although we may distrust these kinds of stories, attributed to the pen of Xanthus, yet throughout Nicolas' narrative of the early history of Sardis, there runs a continuing thread of persistent struggle, intrigue, and rivalry between two families, the Heraclidae and Dascylii. Here we may glimpse a historical truth, exemplified most poignantly in the incident of the murder of Candaules by Gyges in Herodotus' story, and supported by Herodotus' statement of the quarrel between the partisans of Gyges and the rest of the Lydians. Nicolas himself talks of *stasiotai* in Gyges' party. If the Heraclids were the Maeonians of Homer and took control of Sardis about 1200 B.C., then the Dascylii may be identified with the leading family of the indigenous folk, overthrown at the end of the Bronze Age and harboring hatred and resentment until their leader Gyges threw off the Heraclid yoke and set up the Mermnad Dynasty in the middle of the seventh century.

At some time, prior even to the arrival of the Heraclids in Sardis, a famous story relates that there was a great famine in Lydia. It was of such proportions that the king was finally obliged to divide the people into two lots and offer one the opportunity of leaving the country. His son, named Tyrrhenus, was to lead the group of the citizens who fate decreed should emigrate. When the lots were drawn, half of the citizens left under the leadership of Tyrrhenus and, after staying with several nations in turn, finally came to the land of the Ombrici where they founded cities and lived.

This story has often been used in attempts to identify the origins of the Etruscans and to suggest that they entered Italy from Anatolia. There is little supporting evidence. When the Tyrrhenians were defeated, they brought to

34

Tarquinius the emblems of their sovereignty: a crown of gold, an ivory throne, a scepter with an eagle perched atop, a purple tunic decorated with gold, and an embroidered purple robe, similar to those the kings of Lydia used to wear, with the exception that it was not rectangular in shape like theirs but semicircular. This is some evidence, but we cannot go further than that, whatever parallels some may care to draw between Etruscan and Lydian burial habits. Dionysius of Halicarnassus, the first-century historian, perhaps best sums up the weight of the evidence, when he points out that the Tyrrhenians do not seem to him to use the same language as the Lydians nor even to retain any other Lydian indications. They share neither the same gods, nor the same laws, nor the same institutions, and Dionysius is very sure that this is just the sort of story of which Xanthus would have made much. He is astonished that he makes no mention of any Tyrrhenus as a ruler of Lydians or of any expedition to Italy from Lydia as a colonizing venture.

Candaules, whom the Greeks call Myrsilus, was the last king of the Heraclids in Sardis, and his demise was sudden. There are two principal versions of the account of his death and of the accession of Gyges, one recorded in Plato, the other in Herodotus. According to Plato, Gyges was a humble shepherd who stumbled, somewhat fecklessly, into a yawning chasm after a thunderstorm and earthquake. The location is not given, but presumably is Lydia. Gyges is not named by Plato in this account, but the identification is certain from later mention in the Republic of "the ring of Gyges" and from the story itself. In the chasm Gyges came upon a bronze horse and, buried in the bronze horse, a dead man. On the dead man's finger was a gold ring. Gyges took this ring and soon discovered to his delight that the correct adjustment of it could make him invisible. With the assist-

35

ance of this magic ring he at once repaired to the presence of the queen, became her lover, and murdered the king, to reign in his stead. An ambitious move for a fanciful peasant. This story is full of orientalisms and of folktale elements: the magic ring, the bronze horse, the underground chasm. It is quite amoral, Gyges advancing to the queen's bed and the king's throne with no hint of guilt or shame. Plato's source must have been early and popular and eastern. It is hard to imagine him concocting all this in this tone.

In Herodotus' story Gyges is a high-ranking officer in the service of the Heraclid Candaules, a favored courtier and one who has the ear of the queen. Candaules is so taken with his wife's appearance that he is eager to boast of it visually to someone else. He obliges his subject Gyges to play the *voyeur*, a role which Gyges dislikes and in which he is found out by the queen. Her approval of his behavior is less than wholehearted, yet she is attracted to him, or at any rate is prepared to prefer him to Candaules; she offers him the choice of killing the king and becoming her husband or of dying instantly. Candaules is killed and Gyges confirmed in the sovereignty by Delphi. This story must be Greek in source, since no oriental, presumably, would summon a member of his court to spy on his wife, nor would an oriental source turn to the Delphic oracle for a resolution or confirmation. Herodotus has further expunged some of the improbabilities, removing the magic elements of the Platonic story and introducing moral injunctions. He has, then, rationalized the original (Lydian?) story, preserved in Plato, the historical gist of which is the shift of power from the Heraclid to the Mermnad Dynasty. The means whereby the power shifts and Gyges gets the queen and the throne are different, yet the stories are essentially the same, both being concerned with the murder of Candaules by his queen and her lover, Gyges, and their succession to the throne.

About the middle of the seventh century, then, the Mermnads ascended the throne of Sardis. Our knowledge of the political, social, architectural, and cultural developments in pre-Mermnad Sardis, is scant. The literary sources seem to be more concerned with legend and folktale and anecdote than with historical truth of any kind, and though, as has been suggested, some elements of historical truth can be ferreted out, we would give much to find the royal archives or the king lists of which Nicolas speaks so lightly. What is firm is the archaeology.

The Bronze Age village seems to have been typically primitive, but already in touch with both the Mycenaean and Hittite worlds. Iron came early. The years between about 1200 and 900 B.C. marked a period of close cultural contact between the Lydian inhabitants and their Greek neighbors to the west. About 900 B.C. the people began to decorate their own pottery with motifs taken from the repertoire of the Greek Protogeometric potters and their Ionian neighbors, and there is solid evidence for the continual inhabitation of Sardis from the thirteenth to the eighth centuries. About the middle of the seventh century, new burial customs were introduced into Sardis—mounds, funerary chambers, benches—which we shall look at more closely in subsequent chapters, and these new burial customs may fairly be associated with the accession (or return) to power of the Mermnad Dynasty.

II

The Mermnad Dynasts

◆

Naught care I for the wealth of Gyges,
lord of Sardis.—ARCHILOCHUS.

WHAT DO YOU TAKE ME FOR? A Lydian or a Phrygian or something," comments an outraged character in Aristophanes, "that you think you can terrify me with long words?" By the middle of the fifth century, common knowledge in Greece had it that Lydia was a place of effeminacy, luxury, and weakness. But this was a reputation that came to the Lydians only after their defeat at the hands of the Persians, and only after the successful repulse of the Persians by the Greeks at Marathon in 490 B.C. and ten years later at Salamis and Plataea. These victories produced in the Greek states a great wave of confidence and expansionism that amounted almost to arrogance: the power and wealth of the Lydian kings, among others, was forgotten, and Lydians and Phrygians became objects of buffoonery, regarded as faintly quixotic mixobarbarians. The Greeks had not always seen the Lydians in this light.

The Mermnad kings of Lydia number five: Gyges, Ardys, Sadyattes, Alyattes, and Croesus. In the course of their combined reigns, Sardis was brought from a position of almost total international obscurity to one of intercontinental power and influence, not only in a political sense, but also in an artistic and architectural sense. Nor was this progress made with halting steps, but with one huge stride towards political domination and security and with a second towards aesthetic and visual satisfaction. If Gyges was the monarch who established Lydia as a political power of international significance, and Alyattes was the king who sensed the need for Sardis and Lydia to be articulated in some other mode than politics, it was in the reign of Croesus that artistic expression in Sardis and diplomatic and military might reached extraordinary heights.

For men of action power is the only reality; Gyges was such a man. He set his eyes on the throne of Lydia and he got it. Established in Sardis, he recruited a powerful army, of which his cavalry were the crack troops, and he marched against his Greek neighbors to the west. They were to know that a new power was in the making. At the same time he sent diplomatic envoys to mainland Greece, to Delphi. Subsequently his diplomats were active at the courts of the great king of Assyria at Nineveh and of the pharaoh, Psammetichus. Lydia emerged in Gyges' day as a power of international importance, to be considered on a par with Egypt, Assyria, and Babylon. Gyges' achievement was colossal.

The policy of an ambivalent attitude towards the Greeks, with hostility to the Greeks of the Ionian cities and friendship to the city states of mainland Greece, was continued by the other two great kings, Alyattes and Croesus. Both prosecuted wars against the Greek coastal cities in Asia Minor and, at the same time, were careful to guard the friendship of the oracular powers at Delphi and of more secular powers elsewhere. Alyattes was a friend of Periander, tyrant of Corinth, who sent him three hundred youths to serve as eunuchs; they never arrived, in fact, but were rescued by the Ionians, safe on the island of Samos. The friendship between Sardis and Corinth is further attested by the fact that the votive offerings of Gyges and Croesus at

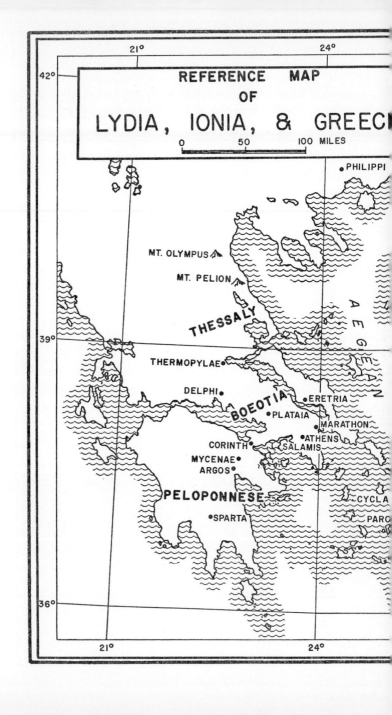

REFERENCE MAP
OF
LYDIA, IONIA, & GREECE

0   50   100 MILES

• PHILIPPI

MT. OLYMPUS ⛰

MT. PELION ⛰

THESSALY

A E G E A N

THERMOPYLAE •

DELPHI •

BOEOTIA

• ERETRIA

• PLATAIA

MARATHON

CORINTH •

• ATHENS

SALAMIS

MYCENAE •

ARGOS •

PELOPONNESE

CYCLA

• SPARTA

PARO

2. Lydia, Ionia, and Greece

Delphi were kept in the treasury of the Corinthians. Croesus conducted protracted diplomatic negotiations with the Athenians and their tyrant, Pisistratus, in 548 B.C. On their behalf he intervened to save Miltiades, the Athenian tyrant of the Chersonese, who had been ambushed in Asia Minor. When talks with the Athenians broke down, Croesus turned to Sparta.

Alyattes preserved the eastern boundaries of the Lydian kingdom in a treaty with the king of the Medes, Cyaxares, and he used the services of the kings of Babylon and Cilicia, Labynetus and Synessis, as arbitrators of this treaty. It was Croesus' adventurousness in this direction that caused the downfall of the Mermnads at the hands of the Persian, Cyrus; but the energy and high competence of her kings in diplomatic weights and measures clearly played a large part in the shaping of the Mermnad greatness.

In their drive towards international recognition, not only of the power of Sardis, but also of their own achievement, the Mermnad kings were most obviously assisted by the discovery of gold in the Pactolus, washed down the mountain torrent from the recesses of Tmolus. The great Roman epic poet Vergil was to exclaim:

> Maeonia generose domo: ubi pinguia culta
> Exercentque viri, Pactolusque irrigat auro.
>
> prince of Maeonia he, whose fertile fields,
> turned by the plow, Pactolus the golden washes.

Coins were not struck until the time of Alyattes, but the value of the gold itself was recognized before that time, and the precious metal so generously offered by the mountain was used liberally from the time of Gyges on to achieve political advantages. Economic power was added to military and political.

The other great asset of the kings of Sardis was the Lydian people themselves: If later tradition has emphasized the effeminate and luxury-loving side of their natures, this is only half the story. Their army terrified the neighboring Greek states, fought the great Median empire to a standstill time and time again, and was ultimately only defeated by a deception. The soldiers were tough and energetic; it is worth remembering that the Spartans too liked to wear their hair long, combing it ostentatiously before the battle of Thermopylae, and that the warlike Mycenaean prince of the Vapheio tomb near Sparta was not without luxurious tendencies.

The Mermnads were aware that their lives and their city required greater adornment and fulfillment than that offered by any sense of political success. First stirrings of this mental inclination can be seen in the great tumulus built to shelter the tomb of Gyges, a visual expression of his greatness and of the city's and, at the same time, the first example of Lydian commemorative architecture. Alyattes and Croesus maintained in Sardis brilliant cosmopolitan courts, where envoys from Eastern powers jostled with philosophers from Greece and architects and sculptors from the Ionian cities. The Greek influence continued to be paramount in Lydian artistic expression, but where Lydian impulses are joined to the Greek articulation, the result is a revitalization of somewhat deliquescent forms, an added dynamism, albeit in a semibarbarous way. Small wonder that the visitors flocked to Sardis to see the golden city, for the Mermnad greatness encompassed not only political aptitude but also a new artistic expression.

The documentation of the end of this dynasty is full and complete enough for us to be able to assign the overthrow of Sardis by Cyrus the Persian, to November of the year

547 B.C. Our knowledge of the precise date of the beginnings of the dynasty, however, and of the rise to power of
Gyges are not as clear.

Cruel and rapacious wandering tribesmen, the Cimmerians, appeared over the northern horizon in the middle
of the seventh century and wreaked havoc on the hapless
cities of Asia Minor. Sardis was not excluded—it was
destroyed twice by fire and violence, events recorded in
Callinus, the early elegiac poet, subsequently in Herodotus,
and in Strabo, the geographer. Baffling and enigmatic warriors, these Cimmerians flitted dangerously across the face
of Asia, plundering and ravaging, and then disappeared.
These events help us to fix chronologically, if not precisely,
the beginning of the Mermnad Dynasty, since Herodotus
says that one of the Cimmerian raids took place during the
reign of King Ardys, son of Gyges, when all Sardis was
taken excepting only the citadel. A more precise time is
obtained through the records of the kings of Assyria.

The Assyrian evidence is archival material recorded on
upright or elliptical clay cylinders, sometimes hexagonal,
sometimes many-sided. These cylinders were buried in temple cornerstone deposits. Of these inscriptions, the so-called
Rassam cylinder tells of the *lud-di* as a faraway district
whose name the king's (Assurbanipal's) ancestors had not
heard, but Assur appeared to Gugu (Gyges) in a dream
telling him to take hold of the feet of the king of Assyria
and conquer by calling on his name. That day Gyges sent
a messenger to Assyria, and from the time he paid vassalage
to the king, he conquered by the help of Assur and Ishtar,
and the foes he defeated were the Cimmerians. He even sent
two Cimmerian chieftains, bound in irons, to Assurbanipal
as a gift. Abruptly (the Rassam cylinder continues), Gyges
stopped sending messengers but instead sent help to Psam-

metichus, pharaoh of Egypt, who had revolted from Assurbanipal. Assurbanipal retorted by asking the gods to destroy Gyges. The gods were with Assurbanipal, and the Cimmerians, whom Gyges had previously defeated, invaded and overpowered his land and dispatched him. His son and successor to the Lydian throne (Ardys, we presume) made conciliatory overtures to Assurbanipal, admitting his father's errors and begging the favor of the great king.

This narrative is repeated in another cylinder, cylinder B, up to the point where Gyges discontinued his embassies to Assurbanipal, recording only his dream and embassy to Assurbanipal and his victory over the Cimmerians. Yet another cylinder, cylinder E, tells of Gyges' first messenger to Assyria and of his inability to make himself understood, since no one in Nineveh understood his language.

The Rassam cylinder is the only one to mention the death of Gyges, and this cylinder is dated in the magistracy of Shamash-daninanni, that is, somewhere between 644 and 636 B.C. Cylinder B, firmly dated to 648 B.C., says nothing of the death of Gyges. If we accept the upper limit of the Rassam cylinder, then we must set the death of the first Mermnad king of the Lydians between 648 B.C., the date of cylinder B, in which he is mentioned as being alive, and 644 B.C. The Cimmerian attack on Sardis in which Gyges perished can be set at about 645 B.C.

The first Cimmerian attack, which Gyges repulsed, is associated with warnings of Cimmerian disaster referred to in the astrological report (ABL 1391) in which omens were given to Assurbanipal to reassure him. The astrological data recorded there give the inscription of the tablet the date of May 16 or May 17, 657 B.C., and the astrologers were proved right in their optimism by the destruction of the first Cimmerian assault by Gyges.

45

Strabo says that Gyges controlled the Troad and gave permission to the Milesians to found Abydus there. He also records that the Milesians founded Icarus, Lerus, Abydus, and Cyzicus. Some chronologers date the foundation of Cyzicus to 675 B.C., and sherds of seventh-century pottery have been found there. If we may assume a contemporaneous development and colonization of the whole of the approaches to the Black Sea, then we can suggest that Gyges was already in possession of the Lydian throne by about 680 B.C., controlling the Troad and overseeing the foundations of Cyzicus, Abydus, and perhaps Dascylium. It is not necessarily a later reflection for Strabo to say that a promontory near Dardanus was called Gyges.

The Mermnad Dynasty then saw its beginnings towards the end of the first quarter of the seventh century. Gyges married Candaules' widow, Toudo, the princess from Mysia, and ascended the throne of Lydia. The dynasty lasted from about 680 to November, 547 B.C., a span of life scarcely a quarter as long as that of the preceding royal house, the Heraclids. Herodotus refers to civil strife accompanying the seizure of power by the Mermnads and Gyges from Candaules and the Heraclids: the angered Heraclid faction made their feelings known. Carian mercenaries, led by Arselis of Mylasa, are said to have assisted Gyges. It was agreed between the two parties that the Delphic oracle should be consulted and that the oracle's decision should be binding on the whole people. The oracle, doubtless well primed by sympathizers, decreed for Gyges. She would in any event have backed the party in power. Gyges was not ungrateful, rewarding the helpful oracle with plentiful gifts, not only with silver but also with a boundless store of gold, of which Herodotus considered that six bowls, weighing thirty talents (about fifteen hundredweight), were the most

impressive. Before Gyges' generosity the Delphic shrine
had received no offerings of silver, let alone of gold, though
Midas, king of Phrygia, had made offerings of a less substantial nature. Gyges' eye was certainly to the future as
well as to the past.

Gyges' first acts as king seem to have been calculated to
take the Lydians' attention from their own squabbles at
home by embarking on military campaigns against Magnesia, Miletus, Smyrna, and Colophon. Perhaps he was the
first to see the need for the Lydians to have access to the sea
if they were to push commercial enterprises. Certainly, warfare against the Ionian cities seems to have been an important
factor in the political and economic thinking of all the
Mermnads. Yet, they never seem to have held a single port
for their own use, and there was only scattered occupation
of Smyrna after its capture at the end of the century by
Alyattes. Perhaps the Lydian attacks, and especially the repeated excursions against Miletus, were simply to destroy
the Ionian crops and oblige the Ionians to buy from Sardis.
At any rate, Gyges' attack on the Ionians had the double
purpose of uniting the feuding Lydian factions and of sup-
pressing the Greek cities.

Pausanias, the second-century A.D. Greek traveler and
geographer, implies that Gyges was initially successful at
Smyrna, but that the Lydians were subsequently driven out.
Mimnermus proudly reminds the Smyrnaeans of their infantry's check of the Lydian cavalry in the war with Gyges.
Herodotus merely says that Gyges attacked the city, and
Plutarch quotes Dositheus of Smyrna who told of the salaci-
ous stratagem by which the citizens of Smyrna overcame
the Lydian army. The Sardians had declared that they
would not retire from their positions of encampment unless
the women of Smyrna were sent to them. The Smyrnaeans

47

were about to undergo this humiliation when a slave girl suggested to the ruler, Philarchus, that they dress the slave girls more properly and send them out instead of the free. Philarchus approved of this, so the slave girls were adorned and sent, and when the Lydians were quite exhausted from their play, they were overcome. Hence, Dositheus continues, there is a feast among the Smyrnaeans called the Eleutheria, at which the slave girls dress as free women. The literary evidence does not support the view, then, that Gyges captured Smyrna, nor does the archaeological record lend it any credence.

A catastrophe is recorded at Smyrna at the end of the eighth century, when houses collapsed and part of the fortifications of the city were destroyed. But fault lines noticed in the core of the city wall suggested to the excavators that earthquake rather than hostile activity was responsible for this disaster. In any event, the date of this is too early for Gyges. The archaeological record at Smyrna shows a period of unbroken development and expansion throughout the seventh century, the beginnings of town-planning, the reservation of land for religious sanctuaries, and the spread of habitation from the peninsula to adjacent coastal areas. There is no evidence to support the view that Gyges captured the city.

Before the end of the seventies of the seventh century, Gyges had moved also against Miletus and Colophon. Of his approach to Miletus we know no more than that he led an army into these lands, as Herodotus puts it; we do know that Gyges' son Ardys, too, attacked Miletus, as did all subsequent kings of Lydia, but this does not prove that Gyges did not raze the city. But if he did capture the city, he did not occupy it. Herodotus tells us that at Colophon, Gyges captured part of the city anyway, but here too we have subsequent references to the city's independence. Polyaenus, the Macedonian author of a treatise on stratagems in war, tells us of Alyattes' ruse to get hold of the Colophonian cavalry, implying Colophon's independence in Alyattes' day, and Xenophanes, the sixth-century philosopher whose home was Colophon, also implies that the Colophonians had until close to his time been free. Lydian sherds have been recovered at Colophon, but they do not prove Lydian occupation, though the excavators took a different view. Whatever Lydian control there was, it does not seem to have been lasting.

Gyges, then, did not occupy the Ionian cities, but, sensing the imminence of the Cimmerians from events in Phrygia, where the great kingdom of Midas probably ended about 676 B.C., he turned to Assyria for help. No later than 667 B.C. his envoys arrived at Nineveh, sleek but unrecognized, to plead for the great king's help. It was extended, and in the high summer of 657 B.C., Gyges was able to repulse the first wave of attacking Cimmerians. Emboldened by his success and secure in his own power, he flouted the strength of the Assyrian by sending military reinforcements to Psammetichus in the Delta and thereby incurring Assurbanipal's wrath and curse.

Diodorus, the first-century Sicilian historian, relates that Psammetichus won control of Egypt with Ionian and Carian mercenaries. Possibly he had Lydian soldiers with him too. Egyptian synchronisms and historical probability suggest a date of about 655 B.C. for this event. Gyges would hardly have sent aid to Psammetichus if the Cimmerians had still been breathing down his neck. The disdain with which Assurbanipal was held by this time is emphasized by the revolt of Babylon from Nineveh in 652 B.C.; but as far as Gyges and Sardis were concerned, Assurbanipal triumphed.

About 645 B.C. a second, more forceful, wave of Cimmerians arrived at the gates of Sardis, sacked the city, and killed its king. Dramatic illustration of the destruction of the city by fire has now been unearthed by the excavators. The skeleton of a little girl killed by the collapse of a burning house speaks fiercely of the ruthlessness with which the city was razed.

Gyges had reigned for about thirty-five years, consolidating the position of the Mermnad Dynasty in Sardis by reconciling the divergent views of Heraclid and Mermnad, bringing them together in a great sweep of Lydian patriotism and political expansionism. Lydian first, and Heraclid or Mermnad second, may well have been his political rallying cry. The power of Sardis was expanded northward to the shore of the Hellespont and westward to the gates of the Ionian cities; the presence of a new power within her possible sphere of influence was recognized by the great lord of Nineveh. Parity with Egypt was not beyond the pale of possibility. "Naught care I for the wealth and power of Gyges, master of Sardis," censoriously cried the Parian Archilochus. He may not have, but there were those who did.

Ardys succeeded his father to the throne of Sardis, and though he was more circumspect in his dealings with Assurbanipal, as the Assyrian evidence has shown, he did not escape yet another Cimmerian onslaught, which, Herodotus says, overran all Sardis except the citadel. This was in the seventh year of Ardys' reign, hence about 638 B.C. In all probability this final wave of Cimmerians may be identified with those whose leader was Lygdamis, who pillaged and robbed up and down Asia Minor until he met his death in Cilicia. Here again it is the Assyrian evidence that tells us of his death at the hands of the king of Que (Cilicia) about the year 630 B.C.

Like his father (and his son) Ardys made war on Miletus and on Priene, thus continuing his father's policy toward the Ionian cities. Herodotus claims that he captured Priene, and he may well have done so, but again, if he did, he did not occupy it. Lydia was presumably in no state to launch military campaigns in the years directly after the Cimmerian attack of 645 B.C., which killed Gyges and destroyed Sardis, and would scarcely have been recovered by the time of the third assault, which devastated the city but failed to take the acropolis about 638 B.C. By about 630 B.C. though, with the Cimmerian threat fading towards the southeast and Cilicia, and shortly to be extinguished, Ardys may have felt strong enough to attempt to re-establish Lydian might in those areas that had come to be recognized as being within the Lydian political sphere.

Ardys died about 624 B.C., and the reins of the kingdom passed to his son Sadyattes who ruled, according to Herodotus, for twelve years only. The reign of Ardys had been spent largely, we may conjecture, in operations of political and economic recovery from the depredations of the Cimmerians, though by the end of his reign he was conducting military operations against Ionia, and Sardis was on her feet once more.

Sadyattes waged war in good Lydian manner against Miletus for the last six years of his reign, but little else is known of the period of his kingship. He appears to have been brave in war but somewhat lacking in self control. He is said to have violated his own sister, called Lyde by Xenophilus, and, repenting suddenly, married her, though she was already married to Miletus, descendant of Melas, son-in-law to Gyges. Sadyattes seems to have resented Miletus' existence and to have exiled him first to Dascylium and subsequently yet farther afield to Proconessus. Later, Sadyattes indulged in polygamy marrying two other women, sisters, and had sons by them, Attales by one and Adramys by the other. And his own sister gave him the mighty Alyattes. A wild fellow, this Sadyattes in whom the Mermnad greatness lay dormant and perverted, to blaze again in the persons of Alyattes and Croesus.

At about the beginning of the last decade of the seventh century, Alyattes became king of Lydia and turned his attention first to the prosecution of the war undertaken by his father against Miletus. For five more years his harassment of the Milesians continued, with the Milesians receiving no support from their fellow Ionians, except from the Chians. Again it was Alyattes' policy to enter the land, his troops marching to the accompaniment of lyres, pipes, and flutes, and burn the crops and the trees. He did not assault the city. To beseige her was impossible since the Milesians had control of the sea. After his return to Sardis at the end of the fifth campaign, Alyattes fell ill and, unable to recover, sent messengers to the Delphic oracle to ask advice and instructions. These messengers were told that Alyattes would receive no reply from the oracle until he had rebuilt the temple of Athena at Assessus, a town close by Miletus. This temple had been accidentally destroyed by the Lydian army in its burning of the Milesian crops. Alyattes then sent heralds to the Milesians to suggest a truce while he rebuilt the temple. Meanwhile, the news of Alyattes' illness had leaked from the oracular source and reached the ears of Periander, tyrant of Corinth and friend of Thrasybulus, tyrant of Miletus. Learning of the illness of Alyattes, then, Thrasybulus expected the Lydian heralds and prepared a deception for them. To impress them, and subsequently he presumed, Alyattes, Thrasybulus had all the citizens bring out of their homes and into the market place all the food and drink in the city. In this way Alyattes was told of the great quantities of food available in Miletus, though he had supposed, correctly, that the city was being brought to its knees by famine. Concluding that his tactics had been all awry, he decided to make an alliance with the Milesians, which he did. He built two temples of Athena at Assessus and, in time, recovered from his illness.

Necho of Egypt, son and successor of Psammetichus, made a dedication at Miletus, an offering for his victory over Nebuchadnezzar, king of Babylon, and for his capture of Ascalon. (This is the war in which the brother of Alcaeus, the lyric poet from Lesbos, took part.) Necho's dedication at Miletus is to be dated, by the war, sometime between 608 and 605 B.C. Since this was most plausibly a peacetime offering, the Lydian war against Miletus must have been concluded by 605 B.C. When the war was ended and he had recovered from his illness, Alyattes sent gifts and offerings to Delphi, a silver bowl with a stand of welded iron, the work of Glaucus of Chios, the inventor of welding techniques. Shortly thereafter, Alyattes moved against Smyrna. The reduction of the city probably falls within the last decade of the seventh century, and a year or two should perhaps be allowed between the conclusion of hostilities against Miletus and the beginning of them against Smyrna. Hence, the war with Miletus was ended about 605 B.C., and Smyrna reduced about 600.

Alyattes' capture of Smyrna is attested both in literary sources and by archaeology. The most striking archaeological fact is the vast siege mound raised close to the northwestern walls of the city by the attacking Lydians. Spearheads, also, and arrowheads of bronze were found in the destruction level of the city proper. A hoard of weapons and an oriental iron helmet of similar date likewise furnish a vivid picture of the attack of Alyattes' men. Corinthian pottery, found in large quantities in the destruction level, points to a date of about 600 B.C. for the successful assault. The level itself is, for the most part, free from later intrusions, and some houses are firmly sealed. The latest pottery from this stratum is of the style known as Early Corinthian with no trace of the transition to the chronologically subsequent style, the Middle Corinthian. Thus the capture of the city took place before the end of Early Corinthian, and the end of this phase is normally put at 600 B.C., plus or minus a decade. Most recent scholarship has suggested that any revision of this dating would tend toward an earlier date for the introduction of Middle Corinthian styles. At about the same time as his reduction of Smyrna, Alyattes also attacked another Ionian city, Clazomenae, where he was repulsed. Against Colophon, and in fear of the famed Colophonian horsemen, he used treachery. After inviting the Colophonian nobles to a feast in Sardis, he murdered them all and did away with the only threat to the power of his own cavalry. These attacks against Smyrna, Clazomenae, and Colophon were evidently part of an effort to subdue the northern Ionian cities, after the failure of his effort to conquer Miletus.

War next broke out between Alyattes and the Medes, who were bearing down on his eastern frontier, and lasted for five years. In the course of this time many victories were claimed by either side over the other, and one battle was even fought by night. They were still at loggerheads when, in the midst of another pitched battle on the river Halys, an eclipse of the sun caused both sides to stop fighting. Taking this as an omen, the two kings were reconciled and made peace, Astyages, son of the Median king, Cyaxares, taking Alyattes' daughter, Aryenis, as his wife.

This eclipse of the sun enables us to date the battle which ended the five-year war between Cyaxares the Mede and Alyattes the Lydian exactly and gives us a firm and absolute date in the middle of Alyattes' reign. Eclipses occurred over the Halys in 610, 585, and 557 B.C., but the earliest was not total and was probably too early for Alyattes, nor will it fit what we know of Cyaxares' movements from the Median evidence that he was occupied in 610 B.C. with the overthrow of the residue of the Assyrian kingdom and with campaigns into the region of Urartu. By 557 B.C., Alyattes was dead and his son, Croesus, was ruling Sardis and Lydia. Hence it was the astronomically calculated eclipse of May 28, 585 B.C., which ended the war.

Not only modern astronomers have calculated the exact date of this eclipse; it was foretold by Thales of Miletus, the philosopher, and his prediction of the eclipse is the clinching factor in assigning it the date 585 B.C. Both Apollodorus and Sosicrates say that Thales died in the time of Croesus, and Herodotus reports the story of his altering the course of the river Halys for Croesus, though he obviously does not believe the story himself. Even if Thales died a very old man, it is hard to imagine his being born early enough, or mastering astronomy and mathematics quickly enough, to have been able to predict the eclipse of September 30, 610 B.C.

Alyattes' war with the Medes began in 591 B.C., a few years after his reduction of Smyrna, and finished in 585 B.C. The Lydian king had thus secured the boundaries of his realm and delineated the extent of the power of the Mermnad kings. Croesus, Alyattes' eldest son, was born in

596 B.C. and was sent, perhaps in 575 B.C., to be governor of Adramyttium and the Plain of Thebe in the north. The extent of Lydian political sway, then, ranged from the Troad in the north to the lands of Miletus in the south, and from the Ionian coastal cities in the west to the banks of the Halys in the east.

Cimmerians lingering in Asia Minor were expelled by Alyattes. They are probably to be identified with a sedentary group of these tribesmen who had settled at Antandrus and lived there for a hundred years. If they had accompanied the large Cimmerian incursions of the seventh century, then they must have arrived in Asia about 670 B.C., and Alyattes probably drove them out about 570 B.C. Perhaps it was for this reason that Croesus was sent north to Adramyttium, either to keep an eye on neighboring Antandrus or actually to expel the Cimmerians living there.

Yet another military campaign was undertaken by Alyattes towards the end of his reign, against Priene and Caria. In this, Croesus served as a military commander. Alyattes instructed him to appear with his army at Sardis on an appointed day, but Croesus had been spending his income injudiciously and was ill prepared. He tried to borrow money from a Lydian, Sadyattes, to keep his mercenaries happy, but Sadyattes refused to help. In desperation Croesus went to Ephesus where a friend of his, Pamphaes of Priene, persuaded his father to lend Croesus the money he needed. Pamphaes was well rewarded, for after he became king Croesus gave him a wagon full of gold from the royal treasury in Sardis. Sadyattes too reaped the rewards of his lack of foresight; he was stripped of all his property, which Croesus dedicated to Artemis of Ephesus. Equipped with Pamphaes' money, Croesus was able to arrive in Sardis on time with his army of mercenaries, and took part in the campaign. No conspicuous success was gained by the Lydians before Priene, and they appear to have been out-generaled by the clever Bias.

After a long and successful reign Alyattes died in 561/560 B.C. and handed over to his eldest son, Croesus, a kingdom at the zenith of her political power, and one in which there had already begun a mighty efflorescence of artistic expression, dependent in much of its manifestation on Greek prototypes but with a liberal admixture of native elements. The earliest form of expression which this artistic tendency took was in architecture, and in architecture of a funerary nature. The tomb of Alyattes was far-famed even in antiquity.

III

Dust to Dust

◆

*But the land of Lydia hath no marvels to describe, ex-
cepting the gold dust that is washed down from
Tmolus: but it containeth the greatest work of man by
far, saving the works in Egypt and in Babylon: for
there is in it the tomb of Alyattes, the father of Croesus,
the foundation whereof is of great stones and the rest
of the tomb an heap of earth.—*HERODOTUS.

WRITING A CENTURY OR SO after the death of Alyattes,
Herodotus records that Lydia, unlike most other countries,
offers scarcely any wonders worthy of description. His two
exceptions are the gold dust from the Pactolus and the tomb
of Alyattes. This tomb, he says, has a surrounding retaining
wall of mighty stones, and the rest of it is of piled up
earth; it was built by the merchants, the artisans, and
the whores. He saw five boundary markers, set up still in
his day, bearing the written record of the amounts of work
contributed by each. The whores' share of the work was the
largest. The tumulus measured six stades and two plethra
(about three quarters of a mile) in circumference and thirteen plethra (about one quarter of a mile) in diameter.

This tumulus sits at the eastern end of the royal cemetery,
northward from Sardis across the river Hermus, between
the Hermus and the Gygaean Lake, and facing Sardis.
Chandler, the eighteenth-century English traveler and ex-
plorer, describes the locale as follows:

the lake is very large, it abounds in fish, its colour and

taste like common pond water, with beds of sedge growing in it. The barrows (or tombs of the kings) are of various sizes, the smaller made perhaps for children of the younger branches of the royal family; four or five are distinguished by their superior magnitude, and are visible as hills at a great distance: the lake, it is likely, furnished the soil. All of them are covered with green turf; and as many as I observed, in passing among them, retain their conical form, without any sinking in of the top. One of the barrows on the eminence, near the middle, and towards Sardis, is remarkably conspicuous: it was the monument of Alyattes. It is much taller and handsomer than any I have seen in England, or elsewhere.

Standing in solitary grandeur, these mounds are mute witnesses to the piety of the citizens of Sardis, ghostly recollections of the might of the kings and nobility, who even in death were turned to face, from beyond the plain and the river Hermus, the activities of the Mermnad capital. Here the citizens labored to commemorate their kings and masters, and hither came the funeral processions winding their way from Sardis bearing proud nobles to their last resting places.

The cemetery consists of about one hundred burial mounds, among which three are prominent, and of these three it is the easternmost, the largest, which is identifiable as that of Alyattes. This mound attracted the attention of H. Spiegelthal, the Prussian consul in Smyrna in 1853, and in that year he tunneled into the mound from the south. He encountered a vast series of robber tunnels, which led him to a looted chamber, and he was able to measure and draw the whole complex. His findings were meticulously published by his associate, J. F. M. von Olfers.

Spiegelthal was able to measure the surrounding retaining

wall, or *krepis*, of the mound, now vanished, and correctly assumed that these were the measurements that Herodotus used or had access to. Spiegelthal calculated the diameter of the *krepis* as 355.2 meters, giving a circumference of 1,115.32 meters, and was able to make some observations on the length of Herodotean stades and plethra. Within the marble chamber and antechamber which he found, burrowed deep into the heart of the mound, Spiegelthal came upon fragments of typical Lydian pottery, and late Protocorinthian sherds, which should be dated in the third quarter of the seventh century. These set the construction of the tomb possibly late in the seventh or early in the sixth century.

In 1962 and 1963 the Harvard-Cornell expedition was able to get into the mound again and to locate the tunnels and chamber discovered by Spiegelthal. Our own observations substantiated Spiegelthal's accurate drawings and recorded for certain that the chamber is not located at the geometric center of the mound, viewed either in the horizontal or vertical plane. The location suggested that there were perhaps other chambers within the mound, since the chamber itself is of much the same size as those within the smaller mounds, of which one was opened in 1962 and another of slightly different architectural arrangement in 1963. On the other hand, no chamber was found at the assumed center of another of the three largest mounds where excavation was carried on in the seasons 1964–66. This evidence seems to argue that the off-center chamber of canonical size which Spiegelthal found within the tomb of Alyattes is, in fact, the burial chamber of Alyattes himself. Doubtless the court architects were aware of the attention the mound would attract, that of burglars as well as of revering citizens.

The burial chamber of Alyattes itself, measuring roughly

3.5 meters by 2.5 meters and about 2.5 meters high, shows a remarkable degree of skill on the part of the masons. The marble blocks are highly polished, have drafted edges, and fit together with astonishing precision. Iron clamps were used, as in the other chambers excavated. On top of the chamber, between the ceiling blocks and the strata of dumped sand, clay, gravel, and earth, there was a thick deposit of oak ashes, already noted by Spiegelthal. After the construction a fire of considerable size had burned on top of the roof of the chamber. This fire must have been part of the funeral ceremonies, but was it simply to symbolize the brevity and extinction of life, or can we see here some real reflection of the Herodotean story of Croesus on the pyre? Hittite kings were cremated, and perhaps we can assume that the Lydians exercised the same royal rite. When the fire was extinguished and either the body or the ashes laid to rest in the tomb chamber, then began the heaping of the mound, a practice of which we have vivid descriptions in Homer:

> Then
> they laid what they had gathered up in a golden casket
> and wrapped this about with soft robes of purple, and presently
> put it away in the hollow of the grave, and over it
> piled huge stones laid close together. Lightly and quickly
> they piled up the grave-barrow, and on all sides were set watchmen
> for fear the strong-greaved Achaians might too soon set upon them.
> They piled up the grave-barrow and went away, and thereafter
> assembled in a fair gathering and held a glorious

feast within the house of Priam, king under God's
hand.
Such was their burial of Hektor, breaker of horses.

Hipponax, the iambic poet writing in the latter half of the
sixth century in Ephesus, urged a traveling friend to go to
Smyrna, turning his belly to the setting sun and passing
through the land of the Lydians by the tombs of Attales,
Gyges, the stele of some unknown person, and the tomb
of Tos. The text is fragmentary and very damaged, only
preserved by Tzetzes, the twelfth-century Byzantine scholar, as an example of his theory that trisyllables could appear
in the fifth foot. His interest was neither historical nor
topographical. What is clear is that the traveler is to travel
from east to west through Lydia to Smyrna, and that the
first mound he would see, the easternmost that is, is that of
Attales. This must be a corruption of *Alyattes*, since, as
Herodotus has said, only one of the tombs is worth men-
tioning, and that is the largest and the tomb of Alyattes. The
easternmost is the largest, hence the tomb of Alyattes. The
central of the three principal mounds, then, on the evidence
of Hipponax, is that of Gyges, the first Mermnad king of
the Lydians, and we may suggest that the stele mentioned
by Hipponax refers to some monument atop Gyges' tomb.

It has been argued that Hipponax is referring to four
monuments, not three, and that the stele to which he alludes
is the stele of the mistress of Gyges, who, according to
Clearchus of Soli, the third-century writer, was so loved
by the king that he gave himself and his kingdom over to
her, and that when she died he summoned all the Lydian
people together, and they built so huge a monument to her
that he could see it wherever he happened to be around

Tmolus. But Clearchus is not a very reliable source, and there is a clear reflection in his story of the vastness with which Herodotus describes the tomb of Alyattes.

Of Tos nothing is known and the text again is corrupt. Proper names are particularly liable to palaeographical error, and we may suggest an amendment either to *Atyos* or *Ardyos*, hence the tomb of Atys or Ardys. Of these, *Atyos* is more comfortable metrically and grammatically; *Ardyos* is preferable on grounds of historical probability. These three outstandingly large mounds in the royal cemetery at Sardis, then, are the tombs of Alyattes, Gyges, and Ardys, three of the five Mermnad rulers.

The central of these three mounds, that identified as the tomb of Gyges, has been the subject of very recent activity by the Harvard-Cornell expedition. In the summer of 1963 trial trenches were dug around the mound and across what looked like robbers' workings in the south and northeast faces. The only object brought to light was a Roman coin of the fourth century, perhaps indicating that robbers had been busy with the mound and that they had been Romans. Attempts to find a dromos, a passageway leading to the tomb chamber, in the south face were fruitless, and the results of drilling and resistivity tests were inconclusive. It became clear that only tunneling could produce any satisfactory results. This was begun in 1964.

The mound itself is situated, almost precariously, on the southern edge of an east-west limestone ridge, and to the north and east the limestone has been quarried away. Due to erosion, the present shape is irregular, with the mound spreading away into the lower ground to the south. Trenches dug in the northeast sector seemed to indicate a roughly quarried edge forming the exterior of the original

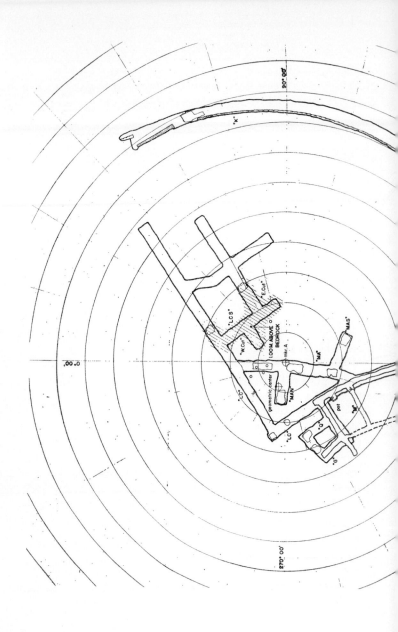

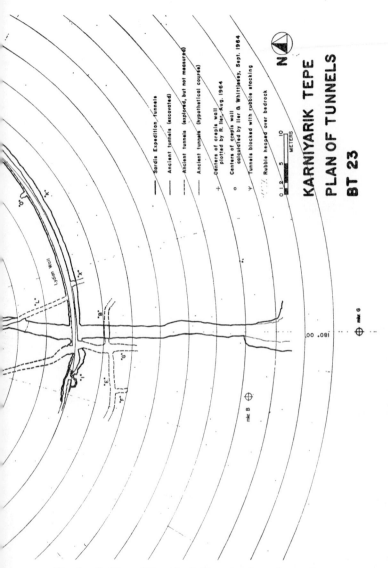

KARNIYARIK TEPE
PLAN OF TUNNELS
BT 23

N

—————— Sardis Expedition tunnels

——— Ancient tunnels (excavated)

——— Ancient tunnels (explored, but not measured)

········· Ancient tunnels (hypothetical course)

+ Centers of crepis wall
plotted by R. Iler, Aug. 1964

o Centers of crepis wall
calculated by Iler & Whittlesey, Sept. 1964

Y Tunnels blocked with rubble stacking

///· Rubble heaped over bedrock

0 1 2   5   10
METERS

Lydian Wall

180.00

mkr. B

mkr. G

3. Karniyarik Tepe (Mound of Gyges): plan of tunnels

mound, perhaps some 105 meters from the calculated center of the mound in the same plane. Hence the mound was given a total diameter of about 210 meters.

The architect could not have known the equation for the area of a circle, but in his drawings he must have needed to include a measurement for the diameter. The circumference was perhaps measured on the ground or perhaps by approximation to a square or polygon. The mound consists of alternating layers of harder red clays and softer greenish clay earth, with liberal admixture, here and there, of limestone chips and irregular blocks scattered throughout the mass. It was these which had rendered useless the operation of the drill that had produced such sensational results when used on the royal Phrygian tumuli at Gordium. Layers of river stones and limestone rubble also form part of the structure of the mound, though these seem confined to the inner core.

A long gallery was driven towards the assumed center of the mound from the south in 1964, and some 25 meters from the entrance robber tunnels were encountered. Of these about 130 meters were either excavated or explored, and some hint of the date of this ancient penetration of the Lydian mound is given by the recovery, in a niche opening to the north off one of the tunnels, of a plainware buff jug, broken but almost complete. The shape, technique, and fabric of this vessel are thought to be Roman, perhaps of the late first or second century A.D.

Five meters beyond the first discovery of the ancient tunnels within the mound, the excavators came on a large substantial stone wall, along which the robbers had pursued their way, and which curved away either side the new tunnel, to west and east. This wall deep within the heart of the mound was immediately recognized as the retaining wall, the Herodotean *krepis*, for a smaller mound, perhaps some ninety meters in diameter. By the end of the season of 1966, almost one hundred meters of the outer face of this massive wall had been exposed, measuring rather more than one-third of the circumference of the circle formed by the wall and constituting the ground plan of the mound. To the west the wall continues but could not be followed; to the east and northeast the swing of the arc of the circle was pursued until the wall stopped where the bedrock began to rise rather abruptly and the lowest course of the wall itself was formed of bedrock dressed like quarried blocks. After a break of about five meters, the wall continued.

The wall is built of limestone blocks, quarried locally, and in all probability taken from the limestone ridge on which the mound itself sits. There are three courses, two of ashlar masonry, rectangular, and one crowning, almost circular, bolster course. The blocks are of irregular lengths, though the height of the courses remains reasonably even. The height of each course is about sixty centimeters. The ashlar blocks are drafted with either evenly picked or rough picked surfaces and carefully worked borders. Beveling is applied regularly on the lower edge of the upper and the upper edge of the lower ashlar courses, and elsewhere rather indiscriminately. Rope holes can still be seen, and two lifting bosses are still preserved on the surface. This large retaining wall was never completed, and the state of incompletion may be judged as well from the omission of decorative details as from missing blocks.

One of the most tantalizing features of this wall within the mound is the appearance of a sign reiterated no less than twenty-four times, in two groups of twelve each, and distributed on both upper and lower courses. This sign is very deeply incised in the blocks and varies in height from nine centimeters to about twenty centimeters. The reading is the same whether the character is considered as being upside down or not. It may be read in a number of ways, possibly comprising a ligature of the Greek letters *digamma* and *epsilon*; but the most plausible suggestion so far proposed suggests that this sign should be read as a monogram combining two *gamma*'s and two *upsilon*'s, and hence is legible as *Gugu*, the name by which King Gyges is known in the Assyrian records. It is the size and the deep cutting of these repeated signs which marks them off as more significant than other signs also written on the wall, of which there have appeared two pairs of swastikas, very lightly sketched and with traces of red paint, a single upside-down *alpha*, a single *theta* with horizontal bar, and a single S lying on its side. It is possible that the signs register some degree of orientation, which would in this case have to be interpreted as southeast, since it is in the southeast quadrant that these incised blocks occur, and the geographical concentration of the blocks with these signs inscribed does argue somewhat in favor of this suggestion. They might also be, quite simply, mason's marks.

But if the identification of the sign with Gugu is correct, we have a striking confirmation of the conclusion already reached on the grounds of the evidence offered by Hipponax, that this mound housed the tomb of the great king Gyges, first Mermnad lord of Sardis. And with the discovery of the retaining wall itself, we have evidence not only for Lydian mastery of imposing masonry but also for the existence of writing skills in Lydia about the middle of the seventh century B.C.

A tunnel was continued beyond the massive Lydian retaining wall for a further forty meters to the calculated centers of the mound, following the paths of earlier robbers, but no trace has yet been found of the tomb chamber itself. Doubtless, as in the case of the tomb of Alyattes, the chamber was located off-center deliberately, and perhaps at a considerable distance from the center, if we may rightly judge from the evidence of other Lydian chambers and their positioning within the mounds.

The existence of a second hill of earth within the mound sheltering the tomb of Gyges poses many interesting questions, of which the historical implications are perhaps the most engaging. The retaining wall within the mound was never finished, and this suggests that Gyges died before his masons were able to finish the job. Hence, we may say that work began on the retaining wall and the pouring of the mound sometime within the lifespan of the king, about 680–645 B.C. The lowest ashlar course was laid and the upper ashlar and the bolster course were being prepared by the masons. This wall was to be the retaining wall of a tumulus whose diameter was to be about 90 meters and circumference rather more than 270 meters. After Gyges died in battle against the Cimmerians, the masonry *krepis* was left unfinished, a chamber was constructed at some still unrecovered spot within the bulk of the mound, and the tumulus itself was extended so that the diameter of the newly planned mound was to be about 210 meters. Further pouring of earth concealed both the chamber and the earlier retaining wall and vastly increased the size of the mound. At some time in antiquity, blocks of the retaining wall within the mound were shaken and disturbed, probably by earthquake, and subsequently in Roman times a systematic and apparently nonclandestine attempt was made to locate the chamber, with no apparent sign of success.

The size of the mounds reflects considerable power and wealth. That writing should have been available for Gyges need not surprise us, since writing in the Greek alphabet was already under way in the last quarter of the eighth century. But the surprisingly advanced masonry techniques displayed in the retaining wall pose two questions. There was nothing of this sort in Greece in the middle of the seventh century, and we must wonder where the Lydians acquired their skill. Contact with Egypt has been seen in the reign of Gyges, and this provides one possibility, but the kings of the Urartu to the east also disposed of advanced stoneworking abilities. Secondly, given the sophisticated ability with masonry, it seems perhaps strange that, with one possible exception, no civic building has yet been unearthed to match the houses of the dead either in majesty or materials.

These mounds, whether of enormous proportions like those of Alyattes, Ardys, and Gyges or of the smaller, less ambitious variety, indicate the introduction into Lydia of new burial customs, the characteristics of which are mounds and funerary chambers and benches. Closest parallels to these fashions are to be found in Phrygia, and it is in emulation of the Phrygian attitudes that we must suppose that the Lydians took their new style of burial in the middle of the seventh century. It is also possible that their introduction coincided with the accession of the Mermnads. Tales of Gyges' arrival in Sardis from Phrygia and the northeast are to be found in the literary sources.

Archilochus refers to the wealth of Gyges in his own (and Gyges') time, and it is to his reign that we should assign the beginnings of the mining of gold at Sardis. The value of the metal itself, of course, was recognized long before the invention and use of coinage, and the sources tell us that Gyges made offerings of both gold and silver to Delphi. That the mining of gold was largely under royal control is shown by the repeated generosity of Lydian kings with gold in later times. Croesus showered the Greek sanctuaries with gifts, sending the most magnificent presents of gold and silver not only to the oracle at Delphi, but also to the sanctuary of Amphiaraus in northern Attica and to the oracle of Apollo at Branchidae near Miletus. Alcmaeon could scarcely stagger away from Sardis, his boots and clothing stuffed with gold dust, such was the generosity of the king, and Alcaeus was given two thousand staters to assist him in his revolutionary plans for Lesbos. Gold mining, therefore, seems to have been under royal control, but whether this control was absolute is uncertain. A newly recovered Lydian coin from Colophon, with baffling inscription which cannot be equated with any of the known Lydian kings, suggests the possibility that even private citizens may have mined and coined gold.

In one breath Pollux, the second-century sophist, grammarian, and archaeologist, names all the people who he regarded as having possibly been responsible for the introduction of coinage. While admitting his presumption in so doing and raising the whole problem at all, he goes ahead to mention Phidon, tyrant of Argos perhaps in the eighth century but more plausibly the seventh; Demodice and Midas, king of Phrygia; Erichthonius and Lycius; the Lydians and Naxians. And he says that he learned of the Lydians' claim from Xenophanes, a source chronologically close to the actual beginnings of coinage and a man resident in Ionia.

The earliest securely datable coins are those recovered in the foundation deposit from the basis of the temple of Artemis at Ephesus. Together with other votive offerings —gold and electrum fibulae and pins, electrum roundels and statuettes, ivory or bone brooches, and scarabs—the coins were placed in the same deposit. None of the objects has been dated later than about 600 B.C., and the coins must be dated contemporaneously. Thus the coins in the deposit are dated by the objects, and not the other way around, the normal archaeological practice. The closing of the deposit took place not long after the beginnings of coinage, since all the currency found in the deposit must have been valid at the time of its secretion, and within the deposit itself the development can be traced from unpunched dumps (small pieces of valuable metal) of electrum through punched and striated dumps, through dumps with a type to coins.

Of the twenty-eight pieces of currency from the foundation deposit, seven are coins decorated with a lion's head. All are of the same kind and belong to a single series, that which was the most widespread of the early electrum issues. Electrum is an alloy of gold and silver: tests have shown that in the early coinage the gold content varied between 36 and 53 per cent. The style of the lions' heads is Anatolian, and the most important formal treatments are those of the eye, the mane, and the nose wart, the closest analogies to which begin in the third quarter of the seventh century and last into the sixth; thus a date for the sealing of the deposit about 590 B.C. is confirmed. That the lion was the royal device of the kings of Lydia is suggested by the fact that Croesus' principal gift to Delphi was a massive statue of a lion, weighing ten talents, and that tradition recorded that it was a lion, born to King Meles by his mistress, which had made the acropolis almost impregnable, when carried around the walls in due ceremonial pomp. Moreover, this lion formed half of the lion-and-bull device of the coinage generally accepted as issued by Croesus. But it is not impossible that other royal houses may have adopted the kingly lion on their coats of arms.

Any mint striking coins of electrum needs a supply of gold and silver (or electrum already alloyed), and to any Greek of the fifth century the place most famed for gold was Sardis. Aeschylus, describing the power of the invading army of Xerxes, speaks awesomely of the stores of gold released from Sardis; Bacchylides, the swooning fifth-century lyric poet, in describing the death of Croesus talks of the golden city; Euripides speaks of the land of Lydia where gold abounds and of Tmolus as a mountain swollen with gold; Herodotus is the one who talks most explicitly of the gold dust in the Pactolus stream. Sophocles makes mention of electrum itself as a commodity that could be acquired in Sardis.

Herodotus, followed by Strabo, implies that the Lydians did not mine gold but simply panned for it in the Pactolus, where it was said that sheepskins were laid on the shallow part of the stream and in this way the particles of gold were trapped. Yet it is hard to imagine that once gold was discovered in the Pactolus, the Lydian kings would not have searched for its source and mined it.

Plutarch records the story that the Lydian Pythius possessed some gold mines, but that he was so greedy that he spent all his time on them and forced his fellow citizens likewise to dig out the gold or cart it off or help wash it. In this way no other activity was pursued by the citizens and their regular means of living were lost. The womenfolk then appealed to Pythius' wife, who sympathetically decided to use a ruse to check her husband's excesses. She had the goldsmiths make loaves of bread, and examples of every other kind of food out of gold, so that when Pythius returned from some business venture abroad and sat down to his table, he was faced with a golden meal. He fancied this at first and was very amused, but when golden dish after golden dish was produced in answer to his demand for food, he finally got vexed. His wife then pointed out to him that it was all his fault, seeing that the citizens had plenty of gold but nothing else; the fields were deserted and there was nothing to eat. So Pythius changed his ways. Pythius was a contemporary of the Xerxes, king of the Persians, who led his ill-fated expedition into Greece in 480 B.C., and if gold could be mined early in Achaemenid times, then it must surely have been mined by the Mermnads in Sardis. In any event, it is quite clear that Sardis is the most logical site for a mint striking electrum coins at the end of the seventh and the beginning of the sixth centuries.

An early electrum issue of coins, of which one example was found in the basis of the Ephesian Artemision, is decorated with antithetical lions' heads with an inscription written vertically between them. On smaller coins only half the die was used, so that only one lion's head appeared with the inscription either to right or left. As long ago as 1890 it was suggested that this inscription might record an abbreviated form of the name Alyattes, though at that time, of course, the writing could not be recognized as Lydian. The Lydianness of the writing, however, was proved when another coin of this series was published, on which the reading is very clear and the last letter is the Lydian *sh*. This, together with the double use of the *digamma*, proved that the coins of this series are a Lydian issue.

Buckler transliterated the inscription VALVESH and identified this name with the river Ales, suggesting that the coins were struck as a commemorative issue by Gyges after he captured Colophon. But the reign of Gyges is too early for the beginnings of coinage, as the Ephesian evidence shows, and in any case we cannot be sure that Gyges took Colophon completely. It is better to assume that *Ale*(s) is a variant, or abbreviated form of *Alyattes*, and ascribe the issue to him. Further, whether these coins were issued by Alyattes or not, the Lydian characters of the inscription prove that the coins were struck in Lydia, and since one coin of this issue can be dated firmly by its presence in the foundation deposit from the Ephesian Artemision to about 600 B.C. (and hence may very probably be attributed to Alyattes), this is a strong indication that coinage did in fact have its origins in the golden city.

The lion type, then, the availability of gold and electrum in the Tmolus in ancient times, and the Lydian inscriptions on the coins, together with the literary evidence afforded by Xenophanes (in Pollux), the late grammarian Eustathius, and Herodotus point strongly to Sardis as the first city to mint coins.

When Herodotus declares that the Lydians were the first to strike coins of gold and silver, it is uncertain whether he is referring to the introduction of a bimetallic coinage or whether he means the invention of coinage per se. Croesus is thought to have been responsible for the introduction of a bimetallic coinage, and by this means to have tried to encourage trade with the Greek cities by attempting to solve the problem of exchange between two currencies based on different metal standards. By issuing silver coins as well as gold and by reducing the standard of his gold, he facilitated the exchange of gold for silver and vice versa.

In the passage in which he talks of the Lydians being the first people to coin, Herodotus refers to them also as the first people to become *kapeloi*, and there is an obvious connection in his thought between coinage and *kapelia*. The meaning of this term in Herodotus is not at all clear, though it seems to mean a merchant or dealer of some sort, and the existence of *kapeloi* is evidently stimulated, if not created, by the existence of coinage. The problems raised by the innovations of coinage and retail trade, or whatever, are many, and we would give much for more stratified Lydian coins, large and small, and for any business documents.

It seems that there are adequate business records now from the older Mesopotamian empires to give a fairly clear idea of how weight and bullion systems and patterns of trade worked in the central areas. It was the weight that was crucial and guaranteed, not the currency. We may then assume that the Urartian and Phrygian metal trades worked in the same manner. If this is the case, perhaps this is what is meant by Pollux when he says that Demodice and Midas were the first to strike coins. Whether they did or not, we wonder what the nature was of the innovation named by the Greeks as coinage and *kapelia*, and attributed to the Lydians, and when it took place. Gold and electrum coins seem really to be measures to pay fairly large sums in portable form, yet perhaps the invention of small coinage is the essential point, so that nonspecialists, mercenaries, peasants, and other people of small resources could use a metal measure of value as well as the large bullion-using traders. A fair comparison may be made to the development from any signary needing expert scribes, and the consequent and inherent limited literacy, to an alphabet which anyone can learn to use quickly.

We wonder too whether at any stage the Lydians and their subjects paid their taxes and tribute in coinage. This would have been a very speedy way to monetize the economy. We do not know how the coinage was issued or what the circulation was into which it was put, or at what point it was put in. These problems carry even wider implications, and we are led to consider whether the Cimmerians destroyed an old weight and bullion trading system, so that coinage was an emergency measure and began as such. Alyattes, perhaps, built the empire on this new network of small trade; alternatively, the organization may still have been old-fashioned with the new economy growing within it. Here we are in the realm of speculation, and no clarity emerges.

Probably, then, the citizens of Sardis were the first people to be small shopkeepers. Our archaeological evidence supports the literary record here. Quantities of imported pottery provide attestation of considerable Sardian commerce not only with the Ionian Greek cities of the Aegean coast but also with states farther afield. Ionian cups, Aeolic *kraters* (mixing bowls), Samian *alabastra* (perfume flasks), and Rhodian bird bowls show close commercial connection with the states of the Aegean seaboard. From the Cyclades cups were shipped to Sardis; from mainland Greece, Athens dispatched black-figure *hydriae* (water jars), *kylikes* (drinking cups), and *skyphoi* (open bowls), and Sparta sent Laconian cups. Corinth exported *aryballoi* (also perfume flasks), *alabastra*, and *skyphoi* to Sardis, and from the Greek colony of Naucratis in the Egyptian delta, scaraboidal seal amulets of white paste, depicting sphinxes, made their way to the Lydian capital.

Here they were exchanged for Lydian products, for gold or silver or electrum or coins, for perfume or seal stones or carpets or horses or ivories. And the merchants in Sardis could offer their counterparts from the Greek cities goods that were other than Sardian, more oriental and yet more strange to the Greek eye. Down from the upland Anatolian plateau rolled the caravans from Phrygia, Persia, Aleppo, and the east, with Phoenician beads, Assyrian glazed ware, Scythian carvings, and Phrygian figurines. It was a happy coincidence of nature and geography that gold should be found in quantity at the point where the trade routes from east and west converged, in the market place of Sardis.

This much, then, is known of Sardis and Lydia in the days of the Mermnad rulers who preceded Croesus. A city and state of burgeoning political and commercial influence, whose rulers continually cudgelled their Ionian neighbors into submission or friendship and protected their eastern frontiers with a mighty army, Sardis existed as a place where steps were already being taken in the direction of artistic expression, steps which were to become gigantic strides in the days of Croesus. Concern was expressed for the dead in the sheer size of the royal funerary mounds and in the precision of the masonry of the tomb chambers, decorative as well as functional. Yet we have no evidence, as yet, for a similar concern for the houses of the living. The people lived in squalid shops and houses built of mud and thatch set on foundations of river stones. A writing system was introduced but was probably not widely known. Literacy may well have been restricted to the kings, the royal entourage, scribes, and courtiers. Gold flowed out of Mount Tmolus, down along the banks of Pactolus, enriching the kings, widening the basis of Lydian political and trading power, and encouraging the introduction of coinage there in the Lydian heartland, at Sardis.

IV

Croesus: Rise and Fall

♦

*Nireus was not saved by beauty, nor Achilles by might,
nor even Croesus by the wealth born of the Pactolus
stream.*—PROPERTIUS.

CROESUS' ACCESSION to the throne of the Mermnad kings
of Lydia in the Olympic year 561/560 was no more free of
savage political rivalry than had been that of Gyges a century before. A struggle for power developed between
Croesus and his half-brother Pantaleon, and Herodotus
identifies the factions for us by telling us that Croesus'
mother was a Carian, while Pantaleon's was a Greek.
(Ample evidence for the presence of Carians in Sardis has
now been provided by the excavators who have found several sherds with graffiti in Carian from appropriate stratified levels in the market place of the ancient city.) Alyattes
himself was obliged to step in to resolve the squabble by
nominating Croesus to succeed him. An attempt on Croesus'
life was made by an angry stepmother, but to no avail. On
the death of Alyattes, Croesus became king.

He immediately executed Pantaleon's chief supporter by
having him put on a spiked carding machine. His confis-
cated property was dedicated to Ephesian Artemis: in the
Artemision golden bulls and drums of the columns of the
temple with inscriptions attested Croesus' loyalty to the
goddess of Ephesus. The principal supporter of Pantaleon
had been a Lydian, while Croesus' chief assistant had been
a Greek, Pamphaes of Priene. So that, while the parties

seem to have been arranged racially, with the Greeks supporting Pantaleon and the native Carians and Lydians supporting Croesus, there do seem to have been attempts by
either side to undermine the racial basis of the other's
support.

Croesus was thirty-five years of age at his accession, and
he immediately set in motion a series of military events
designed to secure the Lydian hegemony in western Asia
Minor. Instantly he attacked Ephesus. Aelian, the second-
century A.D. writer of miscellanies, and Polyaenus tell us
that Ephesus was ruled by a nephew of Croesus at that time,
called Pindarus, and that he withdrew to Greece after
Ephesus fell. Herodotus says that Croesus subsequently
reduced all the Greek cities whether by argument or threat.
The Ephesians' defense of their city was half-hearted or
cryptic, since it consisted principally of attaching their city
wall to the temple of Artemis, about a mile away, as Herodotus says, by a rope and dedicating their city to the goddess.
Even if, as the present excavators of Ephesus propose, the
archaic city was close to the temple of Artemis (and the
city at that early stage had a grid plan), these defensive
measures seem hardly adequate. It seems that only at
Ephesus was violence necessary, and perhaps Croesus saw
the need to eliminate any (other) potential rival to his
crown and to deprive the Greek party of all leadership.
Pindarus' name seems to indicate his Greek ancestry, and
the evidence that he retired to Greece speaks for it too.
Subjection of the other Ionian and Aeolian cities followed
rapidly.

Croesus next contemplated an attack on the Greek
islands, but was dissuaded from this by Bias of Priene or
Pittacus of Mytilene. One of them came to Sardis when
Croesus' shipbuilding activities were beginning and, when

he was asked by Croesus for intelligence about Greece, put an end to the shipbuilding by replying that the islanders were buying ten thousand cavalry to march against Sardis. When Croesus displayed delight at this proposal, the other, Bias or Pittacus, exclaimed that the islanders were as delighted at the prospect of meeting the Lydians on sea, as Croesus seemed to be at the thought of the opportunity of catching the islanders on dry land. They hoped to avenge the Greeks of the mainland whom Croesus had in his control. Croesus saw the sense of this, called off his shipbuilding program, and decided to make friends with the islanders rather than antagonize them further. He turned his attention rather to the Troad where he attacked the town of Sidene.

Subsequently, Croesus moved against the nations west of the Halys and subjugated almost all of them. Herodotus lists them, and their geographical range was large. The only nations west of the river Halys left free were the Cilicians and the Lycians. The rest were subdued: Phrygians, Mysians, Mariandynians, Chalybes, Paphlagonians, Thymians, Thracian Bithynians, Carians, Dorians, Ionians, Aeolians, and Pamphylians. The reduction of these states seemingly happened with such rapidity, and evidently without the use of force, that it is perhaps true to say that Croesus was obliging the states of the empire, for the first time, to pay accession tribute, and that after the example of Ephesus, they did so unhesitatingly. Ultimately Croesus controlled about 120,000 square miles of territory, only a little less than half the area of modern Turkey.

Then at the zenith of her political power, Sardis began to be visited by the curious from all over the Greek world, by the philosophers and teachers of Greece; among them came Solon, the law-giver of the Athenians.

When Solon had been in Sardis for about three or four days, Croesus instructed his servants to take him around the treasuries and show him all the accumulated gold and wealth. After his tour Solon met with Croesus, and Croesus, indicating that he knew that Solon was a much traveled and wise man, asked him pointedly who he thought was the happiest man he had met. Croesus expected Solon to say that he, Croesus, was the happiest, but without a moment's demur Solon said that his choice was Tellus of Athens. Baffled, Croesus wanted to know Solon's reasons. Solon said that he chose Tellus because Tellus had lived in an attractive city and had sons and grandsons who grew to manhood within his lifetime; furthermore, Solon continued, Tellus not only had good fortune in his life, but also he had a glorious death, defending his city and being honored in Athens.

Croesus, somewhat bewildered, and thinking that he would certainly be the runner up, then asked Solon who he thought was the next happiest. Solon was not disposed to flattery and declared that he thought perhaps Cleobis and Biton were. Ready to explain his choice, he said that Cleobis and Biton had been rich and equally well endowed physically, and that they had received great applause from the people of Argos when they had substituted for the oxen who had been meant to convey their mother to the temple of Hera. This public recognition touched their mother, who then prayed to Hera that they might receive the gift which it was best for men to have. Her sons fell asleep in the evening in the temple after sacrificing and feasting, and never woke up.

Croesus now became angry, addressed Solon roughly and wanted to know why Solon made no account of Croesus' own happiness. Solon was obliged to explain, and said that the one thing he was really aware of was the jealousy of the gods, and that it was impossible to call any man happy until he was dead, until he had died a happy death. He explained that he thought that life was very subject to change and that inherent in any attitude or position which a mortal adopts there are built-in disruptive and antagonistic forces. It was better to be lucky than rich, he thought, and impossible for any one man not to lack something. Only at the end could a project or a man's life be accurately weighed. Predictably, this did not please Croesus, but angered, he dismissed Solon, thinking it silly of him to make no account of present success and happiness and to be so sure that man should look to the end of every matter.

The historicity of the meeting is a matter for dispute, and it seems most probable that Herodotus' treatment of the story is intended to be more effective as an example of a philosophical posture than as a strictly truthful historical account. Certainly it is true that in the currents of late sixth-century thought, the fate of Croesus and the teachings of Solon must have seemed associated. Equally sure is the attachment of philosophical meaning to the story of Croesus by Greeks of the early fifth century, and by Herodotus' time we may be sure that the Croesus story was well established in the biography of Solon. We should not imagine that Herodotus is recording as objective truth any clearly recognizable falsehoods. If Solon did visit Croesus, it had to be at the beginning of the reign. Yet the story is too good to be true. We have no knowledge of Herodotus' source, but someone at the end of the sixth century, weighing the story of Croesus and the philosophical teachings of Solon, must surely have made a connection between them, and imagined a confrontation.

After the interview with Solon, Croesus was deeply disturbed, according to the narrative of Herodotus, and directly afterwards while he slept he dreamed a fearful dream, filled with forebodings of the death of his son. Croesus had two sons, one deaf and dumb, for whom no name is recorded, and another, Atys, upstanding and the leading marshal of the Lydian army. Now Croesus dreamed that his son Atys was to be killed by an iron spear and, in apprehension, he forbade Atys to lead the army, intending to divert his attention by contracting a marriage for him. Also, he removed all the spears and iron weapons from his son's apartments and made a huge heap of them in a storehouse.

About this time a Phrygian prince came to the palace of Croesus in Sardis to ask for purification, since the Lydians used the same rites as the Phrygians, and Croesus, recognizing the young man's predicament purified him. This man was Adrastus, son of Gordias and grandson of the mighty Midas, and, though he had killed his brother unwittingly, he was exiled by his father and deprived of all his property. In poverty he came to Sardis and Croesus received him.

At the same time there appeared on the slopes of the Mysian Mount Olympus a huge monster of a boar, who would periodically descend from the mountain to scavenge among the fields of the Mysians and terrify the inhabitants. The Mysians had tried to get him in vain. Finally they sent a request to Croesus that he send his son and companions and dogs to hunt the boar and kill him. Croesus, mindful of his dream about the death of Atys, said that he would not send his son, but that he would send them all other aid they requested. The Mysians did not object that Atys was not to come on the hunt, but Atys himself did, thinking that he would be mocked by the people of the Lydians if it were known that he had preferred the comforts of his new wife to the joys of the chase. He demanded an explanation from his father, whereupon Croesus told him of the dream, and that he had contrived the marriage for him to protect him from the prophesied death. Atys was mollified by this explanation but was able to persuade Croesus to let him go by pointing out that a boar does not have tusks of iron, and that, hence, he would be safe.

Croesus agreed but, wanting to take extra precautions against highwaymen and other bandits, thought it appropriate to ask Adrastus to go along on the hunt as the bodyguard for Atys, and he asked this of Adrastus as a favor. Adrastus was at first reluctant to go, suggesting that it was not for one of his station now in life, and obvious ill luck, to consort with the happier and more blessed of the human race, but that, since it was the wish of the king and the king had freed him from his defilement and given him shelter, he would obey him and look after the welfare of Atys. So, equipped with hounds and spears, they departed for Mysia to hunt the boar.

The boar was tracked and brought to bay, and when they had surrounded him, Adrastus hurled his javelin towards the boar but, missing him, killed Atys by mistake. So Atys was destroyed and the prophetic dream was fulfilled. Croesus was distraught at the news of the tragedy, and the more so because the killer was one whom he had cleansed from his former act of blood. In his distraction he called on Zeus by three names: Zeus the Purifier, because he wanted the god to know what ills his guest had brought him; Zeus of the Hearth because he had received this guest into his home and entertained the killer of his son; Zeus of the Companions, because he had found his worst foe in the man he had sent to protect his son. Adrastus returned with the body of Atys and begged now in all his misery that Croesus kill him, claiming that his life was no longer valuable. But Croesus would not take his life, seeing that again he had killed unwittingly and was the agent of the gods. Croesus then buried Atys befittingly, but Adrastus, overcome by the sense of his own ill luck and misery, waited until the area of the tomb was quiet and the funeral procession had gone away, and killed himself.

The paradigmatic quality of this story, as told by Herodotus, is clear, and its value again is that of delineating a philosophical attitude. As with the story of Croesus' fate itself, here again Herodotus is concerned with undeserved suffering. We should not necessarily suppose that either Atys or Adrastus ever lived, but only that Herodotus used this story in his account of the development of philosophical rumination. Herodotus seems to be moving beyond a philosophical plane expressed in Solon and implicit in these stories—namely, that man is wholly contingency—to a point where he is suggesting that psychic flexibility and readiness to accept the conditions which events impose, changing as they always are, are integral postures in man's ability to cope with life.

Croesus spent two years, perhaps 553 and 552 B.C., in mourning for the death of his son, but he was stirred from his contemplation by the news of the overthrow of his brother-in-law, Astyages, by Cyrus the Persian, and determined at once to set in motion activity to check the expansion of the Persians. He dispatched envoys to the oracles in Greece: to Delphi, to Abae in Phocis, to Dodona, and to the oracles of Amphiaraus and Trophonius. Outside Greece he sent to the oracle at Branchidae and to the oracle of Ammon in Libya. His plan was to test the oracles and their ability, and then to ask of the most successful whether he should war with the Persians.

His intention was to have the Lydian messengers keep count of the days from the date of their departure from Sardis, and not to inquire of the oracle until the hundredth day, thus insuring that all the questions would be put simultaneously, and there would be no chance of collusion between oracle and oracle. On the hundredth day (presumably one hundred days were allowed to permit the messengers to get so far afield as the oracle of Ammon in Libya), all were to ask their respective oracles what King Croesus was doing at that very moment. The only reply which is recorded is that of the Delphic oracle, which guessed, accurately, that at that moment Croesus was performing an act as abstruse as cutting up a tortoise and a lamb and boiling them in a bronze caldron. Although Herodotus records that the oracle of Amphiaraus also replied with the correct answer, it was to Delphi that Croesus addressed himself, first with gifts and secondly with requests for advice.

Three thousand beasts of each kind appropriate for sacrifice were surrendered to the flames, together with purple robes and tunics, golden goblets, and sofas resplendent with gold and silver; 117 ingots of gold and electrum, weighing either two and one-half or two talents apiece, were sent to Delphi, with a figure of a lion made of gold and weighing ten talents. Two huge bowls, one silver and one gold (the silver one the work of Theodorus of Samos, the celebrated architect who drew the plans for the great archaic temples at Ephesus and Samos), four silver casks, and two other vessels, one gold and one silver, were also sent, together with a golden female statue three cubits high, said to be a representation of Croesus' baker, and the necklaces and belts belonging to his own wife.

The Lydian envoys, who brought these gifts to Delphi,

were to ask the oracle whether Croesus should make war on the Persians, and whether he should ally himself with any foreigner in this endeavor. The well-known reply came back: if Croesus made war on the Persians, then he would destroy a great kingdom, and he would be well advised to seek out as an ally the strongest of the Greek states. Croesus was delighted with this reply and immediately rewarded with two gold staters each of the citizens of Delphi for possessing so prescient a priestess. (A stater was a coin weighing about eight grams and roughly equivalent in size to an American quarter. The gift of two staters was the equivalent of about fifty days' wages, say one thousand dollars, for each citizen.) The Delphians, unabashed, returned the compliment by giving Croesus and the Lydians the right to consult the oracle first of anybody, and made the meaningless gesture of releasing Croesus from all the oracular fees. Then Croesus inquired again of the oracle whether his reign should be of long duration, and again the well-known reply came back that he should beware of the time when the Persians were ruled by a donkey, for then it would be that he would need to flee for his life. Again Croesus was transported with delight, thinking it impossible that a mule should ever control the Persians. He began immediately to look around for a suitable alliance, already seeing the spoils of victory before him.

In the summer of 549 B.C., Croesus was busy entering into negotiations with the Athenians. For Herodotus says that at the behest of the Delphic oracle, Miltiades the Athenian became king of the Thracian Dolonci, at the time when Pisistratus was tyrant in Athens. This Miltiades was rescued by Croesus when he made a foolish sortie against the city of Lampsacus and was caught in an ambush. The only possible motive for Croesus' intervention in this affair was his concern to keep in good standing with the Delphic oracle and with the Pisitratids. Now Delphi, Croesus, and Pisistratus can only have been operating hand in glove in the summer of 549 B.C., since by the summer of 548 B.C., Croesus had discontinued his attempts to form an alliance with the Athenians and was turning towards Sparta, and in the summer of 550 B.C., Pisistratus was still in exile. By the end of 549 B.C., though, the negotiations had broken down and Croesus turned to Sparta.

His envoys arrived in Lacedaemon with gifts and the proposal that the Spartans should join themselves to Croesus in alliance, since the oracle had decreed that the Lydians should ally themselves to the leading power in Greece, and they had learned that the Spartans were the leaders of Greece. The Spartans had already heard of the oracle's reply to Croesus, and they welcomed the arrival of the envoys and their suggestions because they owed the King a debt of gratitude. Previously, the Spartans had sent to Sardis to ask for gold to build a statue of Apollo, to erect on Mount Thornax in Laconia, and when they had wanted to buy it from Croesus, he had made a gift of it to them. So for this reason, and because Croesus had preferred them to the other Greek states, the Spartans entered into an alliance with Croesus, saying they would help him in warfare whenever need be. As a token of their intention, they had a huge bowl of bronze made, with figures in low relief decorating the rim and large enough to contain twenty-seven hundred gallons, and they intended to give it to the king.

Some estimate of what this huge bowl must have looked like may now be gathered from the discovery in France, in January, 1953, in a burial tumulus at Vix near Châtillon-sur-Seine, of a gigantic archaic bronze crater. Deposited in the grave of a Celtic princess, this bronze crater is of unprecedented size, weighing no less than 208 kilograms (4 hundredweight 11 pounds) and standing 1.64 meters (5 feet 4⅝ inches) high. An appliqué relief frieze consisting of twenty-three figures of chariots, charioteers, and warriors decorates the neck of the vessel, just as relief figures decorated the neck of the vessel sent to Croesus by the Spartans. Some scholars argue that this crater is the product of a Spartan workshop, but whether it is or not, it provides striking confirmation of the skill of Greek bronzesmiths in the archaic period and of the accuracy of some of the detail of the Herodotean narrative.

Yet the bowl dispatched by the Spartans to Croesus never got to Sardis, and several reasons were alleged for its loss. The Spartans said that when the bowl was in the neighborhood of Samos, the Samians snatched it for themselves, since they had already heard that Sardis had fallen to the Persians. But the Samians said that when the Spartans themselves heard that the Lydian empire had fallen, then they of their own initiative sold the object in Samos to some private citizens, who dedicated it in the temple of Hera, and that after the Spartans returned home, they reported that they had been robbed of it.

After the apparently favorable replies from the Delphic oracle, Croesus began to make war on Cyrus and the Persians, intending to destroy their power. But before he began his eastward invasion of Cappodocia, Sandanis, a wise man of the Lydians, counseled Croesus against this course of action, pointing out that there were no benefits to be won from defeating the Persians since they were poor and hardy people, and that a great deal was being risked. Of this wisdom Croesus took no heed, but set his armies in motion. His motives seem to have been complex: a fear of the growing Persian power and a need to check it before it grew yet bigger, a desire for the extension of the boundaries of his own empire beyond the river Halys, a wish to avenge his brother-in-law, Astyages, overthrown by Cyrus five years before, and his mistaken belief in the oracle.

In the spring of 547 B.C., then, he led his army beyond his territorial boundaries. He crossed the Halys, probably by existing bridges, though the story is related that Croesus employed the science of Thales of Miletus to divert the river, dividing it into two streams rather than one so that both portions were easily fordable. This is a story about which Herodotus is skeptical, and if he expresses doubt about it, then so may we. At all events, Croesus crossed the Halys and ravaged Cappadocia or that part of it called Pteria. He took the cities, he burned the lands, he enslaved the populace. Cyrus, meanwhile, had gathered together his army and, prior to marching to meet Croesus, had sent messengers to the Ionian cities to attempt to detach them from their Lydian allegiance and thus provide a threat to Croesus' rear. In this attempt he was unsuccessful. The Ionians would not be persuaded, knowing the extent of the Lydian anger if the Persians were defeated and their own powerlessness in face of it.

Then Cyrus marched to meet Croesus, and the armies encamped against one another and fought a bloody and stubborn battle. The precise location of this struggle is disputed: its outcome is not. Casualties were very heavy on both sides, and when night fell, neither side was able to claim a victory. Croesus was unhappy about his numerical inferiority, since Cyrus' army was much larger, if of doubtful quality, and when on the following day Cyrus would not offer battle again, Croesus thought it best to withdraw to Lydia to summon his allies from Egypt and Sparta and Babylon and regroup his own forces. The next year he would face Cyrus on numerically equal terms and thrash him. His heralds were dispatched to ask his allies to present themselves after the winter at the beginning of the campaigning season in the next year, in the fifth month. Croesus was back in Sardis by October of 547 B.C. The stereotyped quality of Croesus' military thinking was here his undoing, for as well as bidding his allies not to come till the spring of the next year, he also disbanded those of his own forces who were not Lydians who had taken part in the battle on the Halys. Thus he was left in the late fall of 547 B.C. with only the purely Lydian army in front of Sardis. In the normal course of events, Croesus could safely expect no military activity until the spring of the following year, but he was reckoning without the imagination of Cyrus.

Cyrus' intelligence had informed him that it was Croesus' plan to disband his army and gather it again at the beginning of the next campaigning season. Realizing that his own weight of numbers had not been able to defeat the Lydian cavalry on the Halys and that in any subsequent season he would not enjoy the advantage of numerical superiority, he saw that it was in his best interest to march immediately into Lydia and catch Croesus unaware. This he did and, to Croesus' amazement, appeared with his host in the valley of the Hermus after Croesus had disbanded his army. Croesus quickly summoned the Lydians again and led them out. Although their life was a life of luxury and practiced ease, the Lydian cavalry was the swiftest and most powerful military arm in the world. With effortless ease, they could canter and gallop and wheel and, using their long javelins, wreak havoc in enemy infantry.

Once again the armies clashed, and this time on the plain before the city of Sardis itself. Outnumbered, the Lydians had no chance. Yet they fought with ardor and delight.

Cyrus, still afraid of the Lydian cavalry, decided to use camels to unsettle the horses and by this maneuver he compelled the horses to flight. He had the camels, ridden like horses, driven in front of his infantry, and these he ordered the infantry to follow, and his own cavalry to follow the infantry. In this way the Lydian cavalry were obliged to dismount, since their horses could not stand the stench or the sight of the camels and turned in disgust. Still the horsemen fought the Persian infantry and cavalry from the ground. Again, very heavy casualties were sustained by both sides, but finally the Lydians were defeated and driven back within their citadel, and the Persians won the day.

The Persians then besieged the acropolis, but Croesus, who had escaped the battle, and who in any event was protected from death in battle by the instructions of the Persian king, thought that the siege would last a long time and sent messengers again from his city to his allies requesting their immediate assistance. The Spartans received the messages from Croesus and prepared to send help at once, but before they were able to set out when their preparations were complete, the news came of the capture and sack of Sardis.

Various stories record the way in which the acropolis of Sardis finally was captured. Herodotus says that an observant Mardian, called Hyroeades, noticed that a Lydian soldier dropped his helmet from the fortification wall and climbed down to retrieve it at a point where the slope was considered to be so steep that the approach was inaccessible. After seeing this, he decided to attempt the climb himself to see if it were possible to assault the acropolis from this side, at a point which was largely undefended, because of the sheerness of the approach. Hyroeades was able to climb up, and with him several other Persians, so that the Lydian garrison was taken by surprise in the rear, and the citadel fell to the Persians. Another and more obviously fabulous story, preserved in Ctesias, the fifth-century historian and physician to Artaxerxes, who presumably had access to Persian archival, as well as scandalous, sources, records that Sardis and Croesus were taken by the ruse of the Persians placing wooden idols representing hostile soldiers in the Lydian rear and thus terrifying the Lydians, forced them to surrender. A likely story. Parthenius, the fourth-century A.D. writer of Love Stories, records that Sardis was taken by the treachery of Nanis, daughter of Croesus, who promised to betray the city if Cyrus would marry her. He agreed, and she showed him where the wall was undefended; the city was taken, but Cyrus did not keep his promise. We may conjecture that Cyrus probably made a frontal assault on the acropolis, but finding it very steep and impregnable, decided to invest it. Subsequently, either by some chance such as that recorded in Herodotus or by treachery, the acropolis was taken. The south slope is the most probable geographically for any attack, and Persian arrowheads discovered on the citadel attest the hail of missiles with which the acropolis was bombarded during the fourteen-day siege.

Once the narrative of the capture of the citadel of Sardis is over, Herodotus' account descends into the realm of paradigm and propaganda. Croesus was taken captive by the Persians and saved from immediate slaughter by the exclamation of Croesus' dumb son that the attacking Persian should be conscious of the fact that he was about to kill Croesus. This was the first time the surviving son had ever spoken, and ever after he had the power of speech. Croesus was led to Cyrus, who prepared a huge pyre on which Croesus was to be burned, bound in chains, with fourteen

Lydian youths, whether as a human sacrifice to some god or whether to test the influence which Croesus had with the gods is not made clear.

Bound on the pyre, Croesus recalled the sayings of Solon that no man may be counted happy till his death, and groaned his name aloud as the flames were kindled. Cyrus was curious and asked Croesus what he was saying. Croesus replied that he was recalling the words of a man with whom he thought all rulers ought to have conversation. The flames crackling around him, the discourse continued, until Cyrus became aware that Croesus had said that Solon had made light of his apparent state of happiness, and that he was burning alive a man who had once been as fortunate as he then was. He also began to fear some retribution from the gods for his arrogance. So he instructed the slaves to extinguish the flames, but, by this time, they could not be put out. Croesus, seeing that Cyrus really was trying to have the fire put out, but to no avail, and judging that he really was sorry, cried aloud to Apollo with tears, begging him if ever he had received a worthy offering from him, that he might immediately come to his aid. In a cloudless sky a flurry of clouds appeared, a storm burst overhead and the flames were extinguished. Cyrus was delighted, and, recognizing that Croesus was a good man, wanted to keep him by his side.

Croesus then advised Cyrus that he was no longer sacking an enemy city, but one which now belonged to the Persians, and that he would be well advised to take a portion of the goods that each had managed to rifle, ostensibly as a tithe offering to Zeus, but in fact to prevent any single Persian acquiring such wealth that he would be in a position to revolt from Cyrus himself. Cyrus thought this advice good and listened to it. He instructed his guards to do as

Croesus had suggested and then told Croesus that he could have whatever gift he wished. Croesus asked that he be allowed to send his fetters to Delphi and to have his messengers ask whether it was the policy of the god to deceive those who had served him well. Cyrus allowed this, and men were sent to Delphi with the fetters that had bound the Lydian king. Croesus told them to put the chains on the threshold of the temple and ask if the god was not ashamed that it was because of the Delphic prophecy that he had been persuaded to attack the Persians and thus bring on his own destruction. They were also to point to the fetters as Croesus' offering from the spoil.

When the Lydians came to Delphi and did as Croesus and Cyrus had demanded, the priestess replied with the famous Apolline justification, in which she set out the reasons for the overthrow of Croesus: that no man may escape his destined lot; that Croesus had given retribution for the sin of his ancestor in the fifth generation, as had been foretold; that while Apollo had not been eager for Lydian power to end in Croesus' time, but had instead wished it for the time when Croesus' sons ruled in Sardis, he had not been able to turn the Fates from their course, and had only been able to get for Croesus three extra years; further, that Apollo had saved Croesus from the burning, and that it was Croesus' own fault if he had assumed that by the destruction of a great empire the oracle had necessarily meant that of the Persians, and that he should have asked again whether that of the Persians or his own had been meant. Moreover, that if Croesus had also misunderstood the oracle about the danger to the Lydians when a mule should rule the Medes, then that again was his own fault.

The story of the sudden ability to speak on the part of the surviving son seems to be purely folk adage, attached in basic meaning to the old saw about blessings in disguise. Hence it is part of a deliberate philosophy of acceptance of conditions. The scene on the pyre is reiterated with even more hectic detail by Nicolas of Damascus, and there is other evidence that Croesus perished on a pyre, notably that furnished by Bacchylides and by the red-figure amphora with the detailed pictorial representation of Croesus about to be burned. Yet, in the story of Croesus on the pyre, the great admixture of Solonian thought suggests that the purpose of the passage is more purely philosophical than technically historical. The intervention of Apollo to save Croesus from death by burning and the lengthy justification of the oracle's and Apollo's behaviors seem almost totally propagandistic, and must be derived in Herodotus from a Greek, and at that a pro-Delphi, source. The story of the Persian pillaging and Croesus' reaction to it is again paradeigmatic in the sense that it points out to Cyrus, and to the reader, the wisdom acquired by Croesus, a wisdom dependent on deep calamity. Inferred is the notion that such wisdom comes most frequently on the heels of undeserved or inexplicable suffering. In this sense, then, Herodotus may be using Croesus as an exemplar of a kind of pragmatic philosophy that he would wish to propagate.

The stories in Herodotus of the subsequent life of Croesus, attached to the court of Cyrus as the professional wise man, are too riddled with episodes duplicated from events in his lifetime before and at the capture of Sardis to have any historical validity. When Cyrus was making war on the Massagetae, a tribe that lived beyond the Caspian Sea and which was ruled over by a queen, Tomyris, he came to the river Araxes and had to decide whether to cross to fight the crucial battle on the other side. Croesus advised Cyrus to cross, and Cyrus did so. The disaster was overwhelming: Cyrus was killed and decapitated, and his head was soaked in a skin full of human blood. The parallel to the fate of Croesus himself when he misguidedly crossed another river, the Halys, is clear. Cambyses, Cyrus' son and successor, endangered Croesus' life, just as his father had done: Cambyses aimed at him with bow and arrow, but Croesus escaped. These are tales projected from the earlier narrative, and we should not ascribe any historical truth to them. What is historically true of the end of Croesus is recorded in the laconic sentences of the Nabonidus Chronicle.

Column II of the Nabonidus cylinder, a Babylonian archival and therefore probably trustworthy source, in relating some of the events of the ninth year of Nabonidus' reign, that is, March/April, 547 B.C. to March/April, 546 B.C., relates:

> In Nisan [April] Cyrus, King of Persia, levied his troops and crossed [?] the Tigris below Arbela. In Iyyar [May] he marched to the land of LU . . . . He killed its king, he took its booty, he put a garrison of his own therein. Afterwards the garrison and the king remained there.

Sardis was taken and the Lydian might overthrown in November of 547 B.C. Croesus the last great king of the Mermnads was killed, and Cyrus took possession of the land. Legates from the Ionian cities came to him in Sardis proffering their subjection to him on the same terms as those which had existed between them and Croesus. Cyrus would have none of it, and the Ionians in fear sent to Sparta for assistance. Jauntily the Spartans sent a herald to Cyrus, still in Sardis, to warn him against the possible consequences of any action of his against a Greek city. Cyrus took no notice, telling them to look out for their own evils. Directly, because he was concerned with Babylon and Bactria and with the Sacai and the Egyptians, he marched away to Ecbatana, handing Sardis over to a Persian called Tabalus and a garrison and instructing Pactyes to bring the gold of Croesus with him. Thus was Sardis stripped of her wealth.

V

The Arts of Lydia

◆

Lo, how hath it ceased, the golden city!—BACCHYLIDES.

IN THE AGE OF CROESUS, Sardis was at the apex of her wealth, her influence, and her cultural development. It was not only philosophers who visited Sardis to wonder at the stores of gold, but also travelers and artists, architects, painters, and sculptors. We have already seen that the Lydians were preoccupied with funerary architecture and that they assumed into the native practice of mound burial with chambers and benches, itself perhaps derived from the Phrygian northeast, a knowledge of masonry techniques which was perhaps drawn in the first place from Egypt, or from the kings of the Urartu, and influenced later by the Ionian Greeks. Contact with the aesthetically aware Ionian Greeks was surely at its height in the time of Croesus, and if the architects were concerned more with the houses of the dead than with those of the living, this attitude did not exclude sacred buildings.

Recent discoveries at Sardis have included parts of Ionic corner capitals, moldings of the variety known as Lesbian cymatia, and unusual stone blocks decorated with archaic guilloches and stars, which perhaps formed the coffers of an ornate ceiling. These archaic fragments were all discovered reused in the third-century A.D. synagogue, but they are all archaic in character and style and may derive from an archaic shrine to Cybele or some other local tutelary deity. Certainly they represent work on the part of architects in Sardis who were playing a creative role in the development of the Ionic order.

Perhaps the most significant of the recent finds of the archaic period from Sardis has been that of a marble monument, carved in the form of a miniature colonnaded shrine and decorated with figures in high and low relief. This was a monument to Cybele, constructed with engaged three-quarter and half columns; it is of the highest interest in any attempt to formulate the origins of the Ionic frieze. This marble architecture is purely Greek and speaks forcefully for the existence in the time of Croesus of a court school of architects and sculptors active in Sardis.

Similarly Greek in style are the archaic terra-cotta revetments, of which the thematic material is quite diverse, ranging from a spirited Pegasus to a wonderful portrayal of a purple-robed Lydian, pale-skinned, wan, and wealthy. These suggest, of course, the existence in Sardis at the time of Croesus of plentiful structures of timber-frame materials that were probably both secular and sacred in function. Recent scholarship has proposed the reconstruction of some eight or ten decorated terra-cotta roofs of structures that were built in the time of Croesus. The actual size of these buildings, however, is not indicated by the quantities of surviving terra cottas.

Further evidence of Sardian plastic inclinations in the sphere of terra-cotta relief is provided by the extraordinary statue recovered from the area of the Lydian bazaar. The part preserved, which is one-third life-size, shows what is probably meant to be a horseman, doubtless of the courageous and death-defying Lydian cavalry, who is armed with a red breastplate, a cuirass of plate armor and a staring gaze. His skin is white, unused to the sun, his hair is black and braided either side his face, and his beard is carefully cropped close to his chin. Parallels to this type of beard exist in the contemporary Samian terra cottas and figured vases, similarly to the wide-eyed stare of fixity of purpose or astonishment. He wears earrings. Although there is an element of a bizarre quality inherent in this piece, it is very largely dependent on the Samian material and most probably belongs to the early years of the reign of Croesus.

This bizarre and perhaps barbarous strain is yet more evident in the spectacular plastic head from a Lydian black-on-red vase, where the facial forms are far more crudely rendered. The beard is a black painted extension of the chin, the mouth pursed into a whistling pout, the nasal ridge prominently pinched, and the eyes and ears again black-painted plastic additions in the barbotine manner. This piece may be considerably earlier than the terra-cotta statue of a horseman and should perhaps be set in the reign of King Alyattes.

For marble sculpture, the shrine to Cybele is the most astonishing. Although only of quite modest size, the height preserved being about sixty centimeters, it is as pointed, in terms of significance, for our knowledge of iconographic traits in the history of religion as it is for developments in East Greek sculpture and architecture. Unique in archaic sculpture, this monument probably stood as a dedication to Cybele herself in her archaic precinct, perhaps even in that precinct which was burned by the Ionians in their raid on Sardis in 499 B.C.

At the front Cybele stands in the façade of a temple between two *antae* (extensions of the lateral walls of a building) prefaced by three-quarter fluted columns. Similar columns appear at the corners at the back of the monument and fluted half columns divide each of the flanks of the structure into two parts. The goddess in high relief wears the *himation* (a mantle) over her transparent *chiton* (a linen or woolen tunic) girt at the waist and with her right hand grasps the side of her *himation* and *chiton*, while with her left she holds a lion, of whom only the mane is preserved, across her breast. She wears a very heavy necklace, almost a collar, and traces of a veil are apparent at the sides of her neck just beneath the break. Unfortunately her head is lost, sawed off with the rest of the monument at this point. She wears soft shoes with high soles, and at either side of her two huge snakes rear protectively; behind her on the background a lightly traced checkerboard design may be seen. Closest parallels to this relief female figure are again found in the Samian workshops, where similarity is unmistakable and pronounced; yet some divergence exists, as in the rope-like stylization of the folds of the *chiton* over the legs.

Eighteen figured panels decorate the flanks and back of this monument, panels divided by horizontal zonal registers which had been originally decorated with incised and painted maeanders, of which most of the paint is now lost. These figured panels are rendered in very low relief, are much worn and damaged, yet contrive to preserve for us a complete gallery of Lydian sculpture of the time of Croesus. On either flank of the monument attractive maidens approach the front to worship the goddess, gathering up their skirts with one hand and holding the other upright in front of their faces. Their hair is arranged in very distinct horizontal divisions rather than being in any sense waved. The lions sacred to Cybele, dancing maidens, and *sileni* (elderly satyrs), drinking from wine cups as they run along and carry indistinguishable animals with them, comprise the thematic material of the other panels. The inclusion of

the *sileni* in the retinue of Cybele is an entirely new feature
and may reflect the importance of the Lydian wine god
Baki—Bacchus.

Unhappily, the most interesting representations are also
the most damaged. These are those which adorn the back
of the monument, this part again divided into six panels,
each of which displays a mythological scene. Unknown
myths may be represented in the two uppermost. In the one
on the left, two eagles swoop to attack an animal climbing a
tree, while there may have been another animal (or human)
higher up. On the right, a boar and a lion face each other at
the foot of a tree. This scene may represent Peleus, father of
Achilles, who has been chased up the tree by the wild beasts
of Pelion, a lofty range of mountains in Thessaly. On the
other hand, the lion is the animal sacred to Cybele, and her
constant companion, while the boar is an evil monster
which killed Attis, the handsome Phrygian shepherd and
faithless associate of Cybele, and the scene may in this way
be connected to the Cybele legend. In the central register
on the back, at the left, Heracles is fighting the Nemean
lion, while on the right, a charioteer, perhaps to be identified with Pelops, the inventor of the Olympic chariot race
and an Anatolian by birth, mounted in his chariot, is pre-
paring to set out. The lower left panel probably represents
a bearded centaur speeding to the right, while the lower
right depicts a composition much resembling the scene of
the death of Priam, king of Troy, as portrayed in archaic
art. Yet here a female figure is trying to implore the king
with the characteristic gesture aimed at touching the chin
of the bearded king seated to the right, while behind her a
young nude man is taking a swing with a weapon either at
her or at the king. The identification of the myth is not at
all clear, and an alternative suggestion might propose that

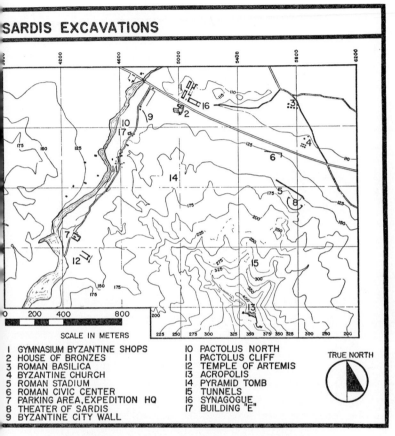

SCALE IN METERS

1 GYMNASIUM BYZANTINE SHOPS	10 PACTOLUS NORTH
2 HOUSE OF BRONZES	11 PACTOLUS CLIFF
3 ROMAN BASILICA	12 TEMPLE OF ARTEMIS
4 BYZANTINE CHURCH	13 ACROPOLIS
5 ROMAN STADIUM	14 PYRAMID TOMB
6 ROMAN CIVIC CENTER	15 TUNNELS
7 PARKING AREA, EXPEDITION HQ	16 SYNAGOGUE
8 THEATER OF SARDIS	17 BUILDING "E"
9 BYZANTINE CITY WALL	

TRUE NORTH

4. The Sardis excavations: sketch plan showing location
of principal monuments and areas of excavation.

here we see Orestes, aided by Electra, slaying Aegisthus, surrogate king of Mycenae and murderer of Agamemnon.

The reliefs all have incised outlines emphasizing the silhouette effect, and the quietened modulations within the very slightly raised relief plane are characteristic of early archaic sculpture. Stylistic parallels again exist in the sculptures of the school of Samos, also in that of Miletus, and in the better preserved fragments of the relief columns dedicated by Croesus in the archaic temple of Artemis at Ephesus. Yet a certain liveliness of pose and gesture strike a distinctive note which separates these reliefs from the contemporary work of mainland Greece or of the Ionian coast.

Earlier than the shrine of Cybele is the lower part of a small marble *kore*, a standing, draped female statue, preserved only from the waist down, whose garment streams down over the base on which she stood, in slightly curving folds. Two large ribbons fall to below her knees and a small part of her *himation* is preserved in back. The garment scored with tiny parallel folds is strongly reminiscent of the *korai* from Samos and even of earlier *xoanon* (early wood-carved)-type figures such as the Dame d'Auxerre in the Louvre. The Sardian figure has the same over-all modeling as the lower part of a terra-cotta figurine from the Samian temple of Hera, and this is dated to about 600 B.C. This figure is only about one-third life-size but shows us that already in the time of Alyattes a school of court sculptors was operating in Sardis, to blossom later and most fully in the time of Croesus. On the same scale but of a different type, is a second image of Cybele in her shrine. This time the columns of the façade stood on high pedestals and their shafts were unfluted; only the lower part of the figure is preserved, but enough to show us central folds on a plain lower garment as in the Ephesian ivories, a jacket with diagonal swinging folds, as on the Samian *korai*, and a huge hand which grasps a snake. This work should perhaps be dated to the second quarter of the sixth century.

These amazing archaic finds from the recent excavations may now be set side by side with earlier archaic discoveries from the area to round out our picture of plastic activity in Sardis in the age of Croesus. The first expedition to Sardis unearthed the eagle and lions from the sanctuary of Artemis (more lions back to back have now appeared also), there is a related sphinx in the museum in Istanbul, and a draped *kouros*, a standing male figure, now in the Manisa Museum, found in 1954. Another fragment of an archaic lion was recovered from the citadel in 1960. For reliefs we have the fragment of a marble frieze from the royal cemetery at Bin Tepe, now in the British Museum, and a frontal archaic goddess standing in a shrine from a sanctuary in the Hermus plain near Sardis. There has emerged, then, the existence in Sardis of a school of sculptors which was a contemporary and rival of the schools of Samos and Miletus in the first half of the sixth century, and which was characterized by a distinctive blend of enthusiastic oriental freshness and Ionian softness. Vigor and delicacy are the Lydian traits, while the formal affinities with the styles of sculpture in the Ionian cities are pronounced and obvious. It was in the reign of Croesus that this school must have experienced its heyday.

The Hellenization of art at the highest level, however, did not mean the Hellenization of life or language. While the presence of Greeks in Sardis in the reign of Croesus and the use of the Greek language is attested by the recovery of a Greek graffito of this period, and while a center of archaic art, influenced by East Greek masters, seems to have flourished at the royal court, the Lydians developed their own modes of living, proverbial for their luxury, and the use of the Greek language was restricted to a very few. The Hellenization of language in Sardis does not take place until the end of the third century B.C.

If the most astonishing creative efforts on the part of the artists active in Sardis were in the fields of architecture and sculpture, there were remarkable achievements also in the realm of the minor arts, in ivory carving and gold working. Homer himself specifically attests the existence of a flourishing Anatolian school of ivory carving:

> As when some Maionian woman or Karian with purple
> colours ivory, to make it a cheek piece for horses;
> it lies away in an inner room, and many a rider
> longs to have it, but it is laid up to be a king's treasure,
> two things, to be the beauty of the horse, the pride of
> the horseman:
> so, Menelaos, your shapely thighs were stained with
> the color
> of blood, and your legs also and the ankles beneath
> them.

We have already seen that Maeonia is Homer's term for Lydia. No cheekpieces of the kind he describes have been found as yet in Anatolia, though we have examples of them in metal from Samos, and from Nimrud in Iraq we have an ivory nosepiece for a horse. Archaeology is persistently substantiating the detail of much of Homer's narrative, and it may only be a matter of time before cheekpieces of the kind Homer describes are found.

From a plundered tomb at Sardis comes a very fine small female head of ivory, perhaps from a chryselephantine statuette. Only the face and ears remain; above the forehead and at the back of the head are flat worked surfaces, on which rested the gold portion with the hair and the top and back of the head. The figure wears large circular earrings and on each cheek there is a crescent-shaped depression, apparently representing a tattoo or brand mark showing that the wearer was a slave of the moon-god. Parallels to the type of earring have been found in gold at Sardis, and similar earrings appear on a terra-cotta head from Praesos in Crete, which may be identified as a Lydian export. An extraordinary example of the Lydian ivory workers' skill, this ivory head again combines formal stylistic affinities to the schools of East Greece with the native Lydian delicacy of shape and vigorous handling. The eyes, for instance, are long and almond-shaped in the East Greek tradition, while elsewhere within the soft outline the forms are modeled in the Lydian manner with great precision and certainty. The impressionistic quality of the East Greek style is dispelled.

Almost certainly there are examples of Lydian workmanship to be found among the collection of ivories from Ephesus. The recent discovery at Sardis of an archaic bronze plaque, representing a recumbent goat or ibex with backward-turned head, lends strong confirmation to the theory that the crouching wild goat in ivory from Ephesus is of Sardian manufacture. The formal and compositional likenesses of the two pieces are strikingly close. A soft outline again contains within the silhouette forms which are delicately but confidently modulated.

The excavations conducted at Sardis by Princeton University from 1910 to 1914 have yielded us good evidence for the accomplishments of the Lydian goldsmiths, artisans whose skill was exercised on the gold washed down the Pactolus or mined in Mount Tmolus. Small decorated gold plaques, rosettes, buttons, and gold strips are all evidence for the highly elaborate way in which the corpses of the dead were clothed. Found in plundered and reused tombs, the rosettes and plaques are fitted with rings and loops at the back with which they had been attached to the garments of the deceased. The gold plaques are worked with open decoration and in stamped relief, and most bear representations of seated or striding sphinxes, some male and bearded, others female. The bearded sphinxes show faces in profile but eyes in frontal view, in the archaic manner. This jewelry is all in the typical Achaemenid court style, and the grave from which the gold plaques come is dated by coins of Artaxerxes II to the fifth century B.C. Another gold plaque, of similar style, only a little more than two centimeters high and rather less in width, seems to represent the Assyrian god Ashur rising from a winged sun, shown in rather simplified form. More than fifty small gold rosettes, each formed out of eight petals with a central boss, and several small gold buttons, decorated either with a raised rim of beaded wire or in a single instance with a schematic representation of a female face were found. The gold strips are for the most part without decoration: long and narrow, they also served to adorn the corpse. One such strip was found lying on the forehead of a skull within a tomb and must have been a primitive kind of diadem or headband.

In the season of 1913 the Princeton excavators made a sensational discovery in a tomb located immediately below the crest of the necropolis hill, the hill which towers upward from the west bank of the Pactolus and faces the Sardian acropolis. There, within the partly tumbled tomb, were found a pair of large terra-cotta sarcophagi, undamaged and sitting side by side on the end couch of the chamber. In one were the bones of an old man, in the other those of a girl. As soon as the sarcophagus of the girl was opened, the skeleton began to show signs of disintegration, but a doctor who was present was immediately asked to examine it. The skull collapsed before he was able even to touch it, but the top remained unbroken and by an examination of this and the vertebrae of the spine, he was able to declare that the dead girl had been not more than seventeen years old at the time of her death. She had been richly bedecked for her funeral. Above her head were the gold headbands for binding her hair; where the ears had been were two gold earrings, and on the finger bone of one hand gleamed a golden ring with a lion in intaglio on the bezel. About her feet lay sixty-eight small gold beads which may have been sewed onto the garment she wore at her death or may have constituted part of an elaborate jewelry chain placed at her feet in homage. The most extravagant object was the necklace or chain placed around her neck and found resting on her breastbone. This was made up of one hundred and fifty gold beads of different dimensions, eight beads of blue glass, and one cylinder of carnelian. Every other bead had a tiny pendant, formed of two convex disks soldered together and attached to the bead by a minute chain of three links. The gold beads were spherical or cylindrical in shape and most were decorated with rows of granulation. This tomb may not be earlier than the fifth century, but the highly advanced skills demonstrated in the goldwork imply the existence of a long tradition of jewelry work and of a school of goldsmiths practicing sophisticated techniques in the time of the Mermnads. The beautifully granulated gold bead found in Sardis in 1961 in a tomb dated by the pottery content to about 600 B.C. also argues cogently for early command of gold-working skills in the Lydian capital.

Many other gold chains, beads, and pendants found in Sardis are now lodged in the museum in Istanbul, along with gold rings, seals, and earrings. Xenophon tells us that when a certain Apollonides, who spoke in the Boeotian dialect, was urging reconciliation with the Persian king, Agasias broke in and said that Apollonides had nothing to do with Boeotia or any other part of Greece, because he had noticed that he had both his ears pierced, like a Lydian. We have already seen that the terra-cotta Sardian cavalry officer, found in the Lydian bazaar, was wearing earrings. All earrings found in Sardis were not, then, necessarily for female use. Nearly fifty gold earrings have been retrieved in Sardis, and they vary in execution from simple round loops, consisting of heavy wire bent to form a circle with the ends nearly touching, to highly complicated formal arrangements. One pair, for instance, is formed of hollow cylindrical portions bent to form nearly complete circles, and each earring is made up of thirteen contiguous spheres. A double row of granulations masks each join of the spheres, and the earring terminates at either end in a daringly modeled lion's head. Such formal complexity speaks eloquently for the goldsmiths' skill. About a dozen gold rings and seals, displaying the same control of simplified and sophisticated shapes on the part of the artisans, and rings and seals of other materials have also been found in Sardis. A silver ring of horseshoe shape, scarabs of white paste, conical seals of chalcedony, rock crystal, and carnelian, with talismanic representations carved on the flat underside in intaglio, comprise the vocabulary of the Lydian jewelers' skills.

If Sardis was one of the cultural centers of the world in the middle of the sixth century in terms of architecture, sculpture, ivory carving, and jewelry, it would be right to expect similar advances to have taken place in the other arts, in literature, music, and painting.

In painting, a small group of vases attest the existence of

painters who seem to follow models of monumental painting and the general style of the orientalizing East Greek workshops. They decorate pots with colorful representations of deer, lions and sphinxes, birds, goats and ibex. But this again was a development inspired by the Lydian royal court, and it does not seem to have had any strong influence upon the popular level of pottery where the simpler techniques of marbling, streaking, and decoration with white bands were practiced, and traditions of Geometric decoration continued.

For literature we have no evidence at all, since the stone inscriptions which we have written in the Lydian language do not date earlier than the fifth century, and the poet Alcman, writing at the end of the seventh century B.C., exclaims in agony that if he had stayed in Sardis and been reared there, he would never have been a poet but instead, an acolyte to Cybele, one who played the cymbals as a eunuch at her feasts. He rejoices that he lives in Sparta and is dedicated rather to the Muses of Helicon who have made him a greater king than Gyges, son of Dascylus. Alcman may not mean that it would have been impossible for him to create, but that he may have been obliged to make wild music rather than beautiful songs. In any event, this might seem to argue that literature was not highly regarded at the Lydian court and that the arts which were considered paramount were the visual.

For music, we have rather unclear references to the Lydian mode. Anacreon, the lyric poet from Teos who flourished about 525 B.C., says that he strums away at the harp of twenty strings in the Lydian fashion, while his companion, Leucaspis, plays the braggart. Sappho, writing at the end of the seventh century, murmurs her encouragement to Gongyla to come along and bring her Lydian lyre (*paktis*) with her. This *paktis* has warlike as well as more gentle connotations, as Herodotus tells us, for the Lydians marched to war in serried ranks to the tunes played by it, together with those of the flutes and the pipes.

The *paktis* appears to have been famed for high shrill notes, and Pindar, the fifth-century Greek lyric poet, tells us that Terpander, who lived and worked in the seventh century, invented another instrument, the *barbitos*, to complement the tones of the *paktis*. Terpander was attending a feast of the Lydians, visiting from Lesbos, when he heard the *paktis* being played and thereupon invented the *barbitos* to answer the high-pitched notes of the Lydian lyre. Diogenes, the tragic poet, describing the behavior of the maidens who worship Artemis, tells us of another instrument used by the Sardians, the *magadis*. He says that both the Lydian girls and the Bactrians who live by the river Halys and worship the goddess of Tmolus, Artemis, pluck their *pactides* and strike their triangles in the laurel-shaded grove, while they also thrum the *magadis*, and the Persian flute joins in the harmony. Perhaps the *magadis* was another kind of lyre, which provided a steadying influence to the high shrillness of the *paktis*, concentrating on lower notes. Elsewhere, Athenaeus tells us that the *magadis* is an instrument played like the harp, and that it was invented by the Lydians and used by them as a soothing influence.

Both the Phrygian and the Lydian modes were accepted into the Greek musical vocabulary, and we are told again and again of the Lydian songs being high-pitched and shrill and sung to the accompaniment of the lyre. Supposedly they were introduced into Greece by the foreigners who accompanied Pelops on his journey to the Peloponnese. There is some clear suggestion, then, of the dissemination of Lydian musical notions, first in the Ionian cities and subsequently throughout Greece. New Lydian instruments were introduced, of which one was a harp of twenty strings, and required answering musical notations; the Lydian musical tonalities were seductive and barbarous.

Sardis and Lydia appear in the Ionian poets of the end of the seventh century. However, they are mentioned more often for their luxury of living and their might of army than for any artistic and cultural significance. Mimnermus describes the power of the Lydian cavalry as it sweeps down the plain of the Hermus; Alcaeus depicts the generosity of the king of the Lydians in giving the Lesbians two thousand staters and talks of the density of the king's bodyguard. Alcman in Sparta speaks not only disparagingly of Sardis as the place where he was glad he was not raised, but also as a city where men of importance and intelligence lived and where sweet and soft-eyed girls control their flowing locks with the Lydian wimple. This Lydian wimple is a matter for concern to Sappho, too, and she wishes she could get one to give to Cleis, all in vain.

The poems of Sappho indeed mention Sardis and Lydia several times, and most often to indicate the city's desirability as a center of power and attractiveness. She exclaims to Anactoria that she must not forget them now that she has left, and that she would rather hear the sound of her footfall and see the sight of her bright face than that of all the chariots and armored footmen of Lydia. In another passage she says that Anactoria now lives in far-off Sardis but that there she shines among the Lydian women. Speaking of Cleis, Sappho declares that she is like a golden flower and that she would sooner have her than all of Lydia, or Lesbos for that matter. In Sappho's mind Lydia was clearly a locale of distinction and desirability. Yet Sappho, Mimnermus, and Alcaeus lived and wrote some fifty years before the reign of Croesus in Sardis, and cannot have witnessed the culmination either of Lydian political power or of Lydian artistic articulation.

It was in the years between 600 and 550 B.C. that the greatest achievements in the artistic sphere were made, and under Croesus himself that they reached a climax. Even so, even in this phase, the distinction and uniqueness of Sardis seem to have been very largely limited to architecture and sculpture, and it is the Lydian expression in these arts that made Sardis a center of the artistic world in the middle of the sixth century B.C. The visual aesthetic response was more active in the Lydian kings than the aural or the oral, and their energies were directed more to the cultivation of schools of architects and sculptors than to those of poets or musicians. The significant and impressive contribution in sculpture was to the establishment of a thriving Greco-Lydian school, and in architecture, to the development of the Ionic order.

VI

The City and Its Citizens

◆

"But we are to contend for Lydia as well: for in that land there is an abundance of wine and figs, and olive oil, and its shores are washed by the sea: and over its waters more good things are brought than everyone has ever seen—when we think of that," said he, "we are no longer vexed."—XENOPHON.

BOTH PLINY AND VITRUVIUS, first-century Roman art critics, are at pains to inform us that in some states it was possible to see both private and public buildings, and even palaces, built of mud brick. They both assert that the palace of Croesus was such a building. According to them, the palace was used in later times as a meeting hall for the college of elders, and Vitruvius declares that the building was used in Sardis as a kind of rest home for the exhausted and aged. We may suspect that Vitruvius has made a mistake here and has not properly understood his original Hellenistic source.

An inscription of the time of the Roman emperor Augustus records that a meeting place for the senate of Sardis existed then, but whether this is to be admitted to be identical with the palace once inhabited by Croesus is uncertain. There is no evidence for a destruction of the city at the time of Alexander's conquest, so that the palace must have stood in the third century B.C. and have been seen by Vitruvius' Greek source then. In all probability it was destroyed in the holocaust which engulfed the city at the time of Antiochus III's assault, when the pretender Achaeus was overwhelmed and killed in the last quarter of the third century. It seems that during the third century the one-time palace of the Lydian kings was used to house the senate of Sardis.

The remains of the palace are yet to be found, though Arrian tells us that it is where the temple of Olympian Zeus (itself not yet found) is, the temple which Alexander wanted to build and presumably did. Although we have good evidence now for the construction of public buildings in Mermnad times in marble, and for the existence in the Sardis of Alyattes and Croesus of highly sophisticated and advanced sculptors and architects, the evidence proffered at the moment by Vitruvius and Pliny is unassailable. We should not hesitate to accept that there were in Sardis important public and private buildings constructed of mud brick with timber-frame arrangement, and that the palace of the Mermnad kings was such a structure.

Although Sardis blazed with marble statues of exquisite delicacy and with public and sacral buildings of marble as well as of timber-frame construction, the aspect of that part of the city in which the citizens themselves lived and worked was somewhat less appealing. Describing the attack and capture of the city by the Ionians and their allies in 499 B.C., Herodotus makes very clear to us that the attackers were able to take the city, but were unable to plunder it. And this because the city burned so easily. Most of the houses were built of reeds, and even the few that were constructed of brick had thatched roofs, so that no sooner was one of the houses set on fire than the conflagration spread wildly. Herodotus, then, tells us not only the nature of the construction materials used in the living quarters of the citizens, but also that the density of the urbanization was considerable.

This literary evidence for the degree of sophistication, or lack of it, in the town houses of the Lydians of the sixth century is now substantiated by the most recent excavations. The deeper soundings at Sardis have revealed that the houses of the common people in the middle of the sixth century were characterized by foundations of river or field stones and floors of hard-packed clay. Upper walls consisted of several courses also of river or field stones, somewhat narrower than the foundation walls, on which higher courses of mud brick were set. Thatched roofing was in vogue. Occasionally the masonry of the walls was arranged in herringbone or potato style; thresholds were accentuated by the use of bluish stone; and doorjambs were usually very thin. These houses were set very close to one another in large contiguous and continuous urban units, sometimes lightened by the introduction of court-like open spaces. The entranceways to the houses were sometimes articulated in plan, at any rate, by projections. Both terracing and split-level arrangements were employed, and internally these one- or two-roomed structures were characterized by hearths and by storage and refuse pits. It was in houses of this kind that the common folk of Croesus' Sardis lived their lives.

The excavations have also given us the market place of ancient Sardis, through which Herodotus tells us that the Pactolus made its way directly to the Hermus. This market place of archaic times is located some one hundred meters to the east of the present course of the Pactolus, which has changed its direction several times in the last two thousand years. Here a stone precinct enclosing wall with abutting structures seems to have encircled the area of the market place with its shops and thus provides us with a prototype for the enclosing wall of more recent oriental bazaars. This wall, as presently excavated, is the enclosure of at least a part of the Lydian market area and is the first real evidence of a deliberately planned major complex in the seventh-century city.

The wall does not run in a straight line, but seems to have been constructed in such a way as to deviate to include or exclude certain areas, as seemed appropriate. There was no insistence on strict rectilinearity, but a more pragmatic approach was adopted. Accordingly, the southwest corner of this enclosing wall is rounded, though there seems to have been a general attempt to keep the wall straight, and thus the space included is rather more rectangular than circular. The total preserved height of this wall is nearly two meters, divided into two sections: an upper section, consisting of field stones and measuring forty centimeters wide, and a lower of much larger stones, presumably the foundation courses, about sixty centimeters in width. Almost certainly the wall had a superstructure of mud brick, since many fallen bricks and brick fragments were found at its foot on the inner side. From these bricks the measurements of the standard Lydian mud brick of the seventh century B.C. may be reconstructed. The ratios of length to width to height are 4:3:1. This ratio occurs at Troy VI and at Carchemis, and, according to the German archaeologist Naumann, the length of the Lydian bricks is common at "Late Hittite" and Syrian sites of the first millenium. This evidence for the size of the Lydian brick unhappily runs contrary to that recorded by Vitruvius, who states that the brick called Lydian has a ratio of length to width of 3:2.

Abutting the precinct wall have been found the foundation walls of structures within the circuit. Although these architectural units use the circuit wall itself as the exterior wall, they are separated one from another and do not share contiguous partition walls. They appear to be single-room houses or shops, characterized again by rounded corners in plan and by the use of mud brick for the upper courses of the structure. The roofing arrangement seems to have been a somewhat primitive form of thatching employing reeds and twigs and clay. Basin-like foundations occur in the corners of these rooms, and these may represent storage areas. Farther within the circuit, several structures have been found, for the most part separated from one another and consisting of only a single room. Walls are made of stones at the lower levels with mud-brick superstructure, and internal features include one or two hearths (in the larger units), storage and refuse pits, and semicircular areas of stones set on the floor, probably intended to serve for storage purposes.

Ceramic evidence from the floors of these rooms enables us to place their construction in the second half of the seventh and the first half of the sixth century B.C. That this area represents the market place of ancient Lydian Sardis is most forcefully supported by finds of large accumulations of pottery in several places and by the discovery of deposits of unused lamps piled one on another on one broken piece of flooring, as they would have been in a shop. These finds and the small size of the structures, together with their articulation as individual units and now with the encircling precinct wall, point conclusively to the cultural interpretation of this area as the bazaar of ancient Sardis.

These, then, were the physical conditions under which the citizens of Lydian Sardis led their daily lives. They lived in houses built of mud brick and thatch, in areas of dense urbanization. They journeyed with some regularity, we may assume, to the nearby market place, surrounded by its precinct wall. There they bartered and bought or made and sold whatever they desired. Only about 5 or 6 per cent of the sixth-century city has been excavated, but we may conjecture that the population in the time of Croesus numbered close to fifty thousand.

To the immediate east and south of the Lydian city rose the acropolis itself, a northward projecting spur of the Tmolus range, high, reassuring, and allegedly impregnable. Today the acropolis is still geographically and aesthetically commanding, and preserved in the central of its three heights we have excellent evidence for the Byzantine citadel and for the massive walls of the Byzantine phase. Much Byzantine masonry and several identifiable structures of that period are visible too on the southernmost of the three heights. Although the whole contour of the hilltop has been altered radically by landslides in the Middle Ages, we can still discern traces of Lydian building in the northernmost height, that which faces across the plain of the Hermus towards the royal cemetery. There a limestone terrace of finely tooled masonry bears closest resemblance to the careful and precise work of the masonry of the chambers of the Lydian cemetery, and a burned stratum immediately outside the terrace contained an attractive bronze archaic relief of a boar. Some six or seven courses of this masonry are preserved, and scholars suggest that this may have been part of the Lydian citadel palace with a stone terrace and exterior staircase formally analogous to the terraces and staircases of Persian palaces. This is the only evidence we now have of Lydian secular non-funerary architecture in its original condition. Several intriguing tunnels have been found leading down the north face of the acropolis, and though there is no certainty yet and excavation is perilous to the acrophobic, these are most probably Lydian. Their purpose remains obscure, unless they provided access for besieged soldiers to the flank and rear of the besiegers or, perhaps, led to a hidden source of water.

North of Sardis and beyond the Hermus lies the cemetery of the Lydian kings, located, as Strabo says, on the shores of Lake Coloe and forty stades from Sardis itself. The identification of the mounds situated there with the royal cemetery, and particularly of the three principal mounds with those of historical Lydian kings, has been shown already, and it remains to consider the other tombs in this cemetery, tombs which, if not royal, at any rate bear vivid witness to the riches of the Lydian nobility. About one hundred of these mounds exist, and most, if not all, have been opened by grave robbers, and a few by archaeologists.

The travelers of the eighteenth and nineteenth centuries, Chandler, Hamilton, and Texier, recognized in these mounds the tombs discussed by Strabo, and their descriptions, more precise than those of the ancients, have given us a good idea of their exterior features. But the interior of these monuments was long unknown, since explorers did not care to face the uncertainties of excavation beneath great masses of earth. Spiegelthal was the first to undertake to sound one of the tombs, and he chose as his target the largest of them all, the one which today we identify with that of Alyattes. His and subsequent discoveries within this mound have already been discussed; it remained for Auguste Choisy, famed French author of many architectural studies in the nineteenth century, to give us the first definite information on the interior arrangement of the smaller mounds. Journeying to Sardis in 1875, Choisy found many of these smaller mounds opened and cleared, and while confessing his ignorance of the time of their discovery or the names of their discoverers, he proceeded to note his observations. Mr. George Dennis, the British consul in Smyrna and noted Etruscan scholar, excavated in the cemetery in 1882 and opened at least three of the smaller mounds. He left no report in print, however, and for a record of his excavations in the cemetery, we have to turn to a letter written by Mr. Francis H. Bacon, one of the excavators of Assos, to Professor Charles Eliot Norton of Harvard University, after he had visited Dennis' camp. Butler and Shear, the Princeton excavators, opened two mounds in the season of 1914, and most recently the Harvard-Cornell expedition has excavated and drawn others.

Broadly speaking, the chambers within the mounds fall into two categories: those which are endowed with a dromos, or entrance passage, and those which are not. Of those which have a dromos, some seem also to have had an antechamber to the chamber itself, thus displaying a tripartite form, yet some of those which do not have a dromos, also seem to have lacked a door, and the corpse must have been lowered into position before the sealing of the chamber from above. The chamber was placed under a cone-shaped mound of earth, and it is interesting that over-all measurements of all these chambers do not vary much one from another, nor are they significantly smaller than the chamber within the mound of Alyattes. The importance of the person buried was indicated by the amount of earth poured on top of the chamber.

The walls of longer dimension of the chamber are sometimes oriented east-west, sometimes north-south, with no apparent significance attached to any particular orientation. Walls are made of cut stone, most frequently of local limestone, though Bacon's letter describes stone that sounds very much like marble, as we know the chamber of Alyattes was. The ceilings are of large slabs, and when a door was used it was in the south wall. (Closed by a monolithic slab, the door leads either to an antechamber or to the dromos when these features are present.) The dromos is of varying length and is most often closed at its end by a mass of rubble or river stones. The walls of the chamber are beautifully finished, and the dromos consists of sections which become progressively poorer in execution the farther they are from the sepulchral chamber.

Details may best be taken, perhaps, from two of those most recently excavated. Located some 800 meters southwest of the calculated center of the mound of Alyattes, one Lydian chamber tomb had a dromos about 4½ meters long. Although the earth that had been poured on top of the chamber had been much carried down by rain water and the passage of time, and the profile of the mound altered at the other extremity by impinging agriculturalization, it was still possible to assume a pristine diameter for this mound at its base of some 35 meters. The dromos measured about 1.10 meters in width, its walls were about 1.75 meters high, of rough-trimmed masonry, and there was no evidence that it had been roofed. The floor was made up of a layer of crushed limestone chips (presumably taken from the working of the limestone blocks for the structure itself) that ran beneath the walls. At its southern end the dromos was closed by a barrier of river stones.

The dromos led at its northern end to an antechamber built of limestone masonry with fine-picked finish to the surface and with drafted edges. Floor and ceiling consist of very large blocks. A doorway gave access to this antechamber from the dromos; another door led to the chamber itself, and this door was originally closed by a massive block found fallen in the antechamber.

The walls, floor, and ceiling of the chamber are of fine masonry, the three courses of the side walls being of identical height; surfaces are coated with a thin layer of fine lime stucco. Clamps were used to fasten the floor blocks to one another and were also used in the antechamber. These are of the swallow-tail variety, of iron leaded into position. The chamber measures 2.47 meters in length, 2.10 meters in width, and 2.16 in height. The east and west walls at the northern end of the chamber display by discoloration that a rectangular object was fitted against them, and this we may presume to have been the funerary couch, of the type that Bacon describes being found by Dennis and that spoken of by Choisy. Bacon writes that the couch was situated against the rear wall and opposite the door and that it consisted of a heavy slab supported on two upright blocks, all carefully fitted together. According to Bacon, Dennis found skeletons on top of these couches and the remains of pots scattered around the couch on the floor. Fragments of a low limestone slab were found in the chamber of the tomb near the Alyattes mound, and may well have formed part of the original funerary couch. The associated pottery and the similarity to the precise masonry techniques used in the chamber of Alyattes suggest a date in the sixth century for this tomb.

Another chamber tomb, recently located, displays characteristics of the other category of Lydian chamber tombs. It has neither dromos nor door, and the proportions are rather more attenuated than the chamber already described. Oriented east-west and not north-south, the chamber measures 2.87 meters in length, 1.35 meters in width, and

1.35 meters in height. Built of local limestone, the walls have three courses of masonry, rough-hewn on the exterior, but the interior surfaces have drafted edges. Within the chamber was discovered evidence for another kind of funerary couch, a wooden variety, of which three boards were recovered and for which holes had been cut into the floor of the chamber. These rectangular hollows were presumably to receive the legs of the couch. Remaining pottery suggested a sixth-century date for this burial also.

Both of these recently opened chamber tombs had already received the attentions of earlier and probably clandestine visitors, and what the wealth of their funerary deposits was is impossible to conjecture. Dennis is said to have been so disappointed after his diggings in the cemetery that he exclaimed that he believed that every single one of the tombs had already been opened. Choisy declared that the sepulchral chamber was never in the center of the mound but always near the edge. He implied that this was to facilitate the construction of the mound, and that there were two squads of laborers at work, one busying itself with the heaping of the mound while off to one side the other constructed the chamber. Bacon records Dennis' view that the chambers were put off-center for the purpose of concealment, a notion which must readily have occurred to Dennis after his frustrating attempts on the second of his mounds, where he honeycombed the hill with tunnels and shafts only to find the chamber at last on one side but only a foot or two from the surface. Whatever the reasons for locating the chambers off any central axis in the mound, no chamber has yet been found unplundered, and it seems that the persistence of grave robbers has proven too much for the ingenuity of the Lydian architects, and all too frustrating for modern archaeologists.

These chambers, of marble and limestone, hidden deep within the high-piled earth, clay, and stones of their mounds, represent the dwelling places of the Lydian nobility after death. Highly advanced in their masonry techniques, they prove to us that the Lydian noble, ready and anxious to see public buildings and shrines built in glorious marble bedecking his home city of Sardis, was more concerned in his private life for the homes of the dead than he was for the homes of the living. It was important for him that his death should carry some architectural articulation, that from the heights of Sardis, men should be able to see beyond the Hermus and in the cemetery of the elders another mound, in whose chamber he would have been interred, from which he in turn, facing in death the Sardis he had inhabited and loved, might be able to offer some protective or remindful influence to his sons and successor.

Less ambitious but more numerous by far than the burial mounds of the Bin Tepe are the chamber tombs of the less wealthy of the Sardians. About one thousand of these tombs, which riddle the hillsides around Sardis and especially those to the west of the Pactolus, were opened by Butler and the members of the Princeton expedition. The location of the tombs was signaled by tall, upright grave stelai, decorated with floral motifs atop and below with painted or incised inscriptions. A dromos led from the stele to a door about six feet high, blocked by a slab or slabs of stone. The burial chamber itself, cut out of the solid clay or rock, had a pointed, double-pitched ceiling; funeral couches, similarly cut straight out of the clay or rock, were at either side and at the back. Terra-cotta sarcophagi, painted red, white, and black, usually sat on these couches, but occasionally, in a more elaborate tomb, the sarcophagus was made of limestone and embedded in the floor. Many of these tombs were reused in Persian, Hellenistic, and Roman times, but the earliest date to the seventh century B.C., and this is the type of tomb which was characteristic of the burial place of the citizen of Sardis in the age of Croesus. Less rich than those buried in the royal cemetery they may have been, but it is from these tombs that the exquisite examples of Lydian goldwork and jewelry have come.

It is not easy to discern what the religious beliefs and superstitions of the Lydians of the Mermnad era were, and though the tomb mounds show considerable concern for the living after their death, this does not by any means imply a belief in another life after the grave. Herodotus tells us of a temple of Cybele in Sardis before the Ionian attack of 499 B.C., and the archaeologists have now given us a sculptured representation of the façade of this temple, perhaps, with the goddess standing in the forefront. Hipponax mentions the Lydian gods Candaules, whom he equates with the Greek Hermes, and Malis. The later Greek and Roman inscriptions speak fully of the invasion of Sardian religious practice by the whole Greek pantheon—Athena, Artemis, Apollo, Asclepius, Dionysus, Hermes, and Zeus, though Artemis noticeably preponderates. The inscriptions written on stone in the Lydian language, though they do not date from the Mermnad era, again substantiate the leading role that Artemis played in the religious beliefs of the Sardians, with varied invocations to the different "Artemides" of Coloe, Sardis, Ephesus, and Smyrna. Other gods who appear in the Lydian pantheon, as discernible in the Lydian inscriptions, are the Lydian Zeus, the Babylonian Samas and Marduk, and an unknown deity, Kuoad. These stone inscriptions normally record the request on the part of the writer that the god or goddess protect the grave of the dead, or are dedicatory in character. Most seem to date from the fifth and fourth centuries. Frequently simply "a god" seems to be mentioned. The Lydian Zeus is attested also in the literary sources where he appears as Zeus Ombrios, and in a recently retrieved *dipinto* on a fragment of a Lydian black-on-red jug. There he appears as *lev*, or *lef* (the Lydian word for Zeus), and the object bearing the *dipinto* is dedicated to him.

Alcman in the seventh century had exclaimed his relief that he had not been raised in Sardis to be a eunuch for Cybele, and we may assume that she was one of the leading deities to whom the Sardians of Croesus' day did reverence. Artemis was another. We now know that the magnificent temple dedicated both to her and to Zeus is a Seleucid building, constructed in the third century B.C.; but a new inscription from Ephesus speaks of the temple or sanctuary of Artemis at Sardis, founded by the Ephesians, and this inscription dates from the final quarter of the fourth century, hence giving us a date for the existence in Sardis of a shrine to Artemis earlier than the overpowering Hellenistic structure. The antiquity of the cult of Artemis, and specifically of Ephesian Artemis, is further attested for us by the fourth-century B.C. comic poet Autocrates, who writes of delightful Lydian girls dancing lightly this way and that, clapping their hands in ecstasy, tossing their heads and gamboling before the Artemis of Ephesus; and also by Aristophanes, who speaks of Lydian maidens praying piously to Artemis in her temple at Ephesus. Croesus himself gave some of the columns of the archaic Ephesian Artemision. His continual embassies to the oracle at Delphi might argue for a preoccupation on his part with Apollo, in whose oracle he put so much trust, and we should not neglect the obvious connection in Greek thought between Artemis and Apollo; but Croesus was too much of a political animal, one suspects, to have had any frenetic religious fervor towards Delphi, and his attitudes in that direction were largely pragmatic and political.

Cybele and Artemis seem to have been the most significant gods from the point of view of the Sardian citizens, and the sources reflect quite fully the kind of respect and devotion they required. There is much talk of long-haired priests, castrated and shrieking wildly in transports of some kind of transcendental experience. They rest and dedicate to the great mother their jangling tambourines, their flagellating whips, their noisy cymbals, and locks of their scented hair. Associated with this kind of religious experience, both in the minds of Lydians and Greeks, was the god Bacchus. The most expressive witness to this god's involvement in Sardian religion is found, of course, in Euripides, where Bacchus himself declares that his fatherland is Lydia and that it is from Tmolus, the bulwark of Lydia, that he has come to Greece with his cymbals and his sorcery. These three, then, Cybele, Artemis, and Bacchus, formed the focus to which the religious attention of the Sardian citizens was directed.

Mermnad Sardis was famed in antiquity for its luxury and laxity of living, and its citizens are said to have enjoyed physical pleasures of the highest refinement. If they stinted themselves in the construction of their homes, there were other adornments of the private life that were not so readily neglected.

Connoisseurs of wine and devotees of Bacchus, they wanted their wine to share alike of sweetness and fragrance and mixed a concoction known as nectar, a blend of wine, honey, and flowers that smelled sweet. The chef Archestratus advised that every household have a Lydian baker since they, better than any others, knew how to make every kind of bread. Gastronomic opinions about the excellence of the Sardian chestnut varied: Philotimus declared that it was too hard to digest but Diphilus, the fourth-century comic poet, maintained that it was nourishing and had delightful flavor. There was no such division of opinion about the worth of the Lydian figs: with a reddish tint and similar to the figs of Paros, they were called "blood-figs," and tasted excellent.

The Lydians were the first to invent the spiced gravy called *karyke*. They also spoke of a dish called *kandaulos*, of which there were three varieties, and Hegesippus of Tarentum says that one of these was made of boiled meat, bread crumbs, Phrygian cheese, and fatty broth. There is plenty of evidence that this was a famous gastronomic treat, and Athenaeus tells us that while an Arcadian could be overwhelmed by oysters, so could an Ionian, fat with wealth, be overcome by the *kandaulos* and other foods that promote desire. Others took a more puritanical view of the dish: Timon of Phlius, the third-century writer of lampoons, declared his preference for the meager lentil soup of his Greek poverty to either the barley cakes of Teos, another archaic stimulus to the practiced palate, or the spiced gravy of Sardis. Menander, on the other hand, reprimanded any cook who had not made the rich *kandaulos* or the sauces usually mixed with it, which are made of honey, sifted flour, and eggs.

Interesting archaeological light has now been shed on this term *kandaulos*. From Lydian levels at Sardis, a series of pot hoards, or separate sets of crockery, have been recovered. These sets consisted of four pieces, a streaked or glazed Lydian *skyphos*, a black-on-red bowl, a "gold dust" round-mouth jar with vertical handle, and a trefoil jug with lower body reserved. Close by the sets of pottery, in several instances, an iron knife was found, and in at least eleven instances the jars contained the skeletons of tiny animals, now positively identified as new-born puppies.

Hipponax spoke of a Lydian god called "Hermes, the Dog Throttler," and a recent suggestion has proposed that "Hermes, the Dog Throttler, in Maeonian Candaules" may be an Indo-European war-god, sometimes worshipped in the guise of a wolf. In this case, it may be possible to interpret the groups of vessels as evidence for a ritual meal suddenly abandoned. Alternatively, the hoards of pottery may have been deliberately buried. If the theory of the prepared meal is accepted, we may suggest that the Sardians from time to time held a ritual meal throughout the city, in honor of Hermes, the Dog Throttler, otherwise known as Candaules; furthermore, that this meal, an important part of which was dog meat, is to be associated with the famed Lydian dish of the *kandaulos*, a part of which, as Hegesippus says, was boiled meat. Other archaeological evidence from the floors of houses in Sardis indicates that the citizens included bird, pig, bovid (*Bos taurus*), sheep, and goat in their menu.

The comic poet Plato tells us that the Sardians dressed in red for dinner and that they reclined in elegance on couches with ivory feet and purple upholstery. Aristophanes says that the floors of their houses were decked with Persian rugs. Conversely, Heracleides of Cumae informs us that the Persian nobility was fond of Sardian carpets and that the king would walk only on one which no one else had trod. Alexis, writing in the fourth century, and subsequently Vergil, tells us how fond the Sardians were of perfume and how they exported their saffron far and wide. It was carried in small ceramic jars known as *lydions*. Some claimed that it was more chic to know of the baccharis ointments, the perfumes and cosmetics of Sardis which help the skin, than it was to know of the manner of life in the Peloponnese. In the classical age, in fact, the image of Lydia and Sardis came to be identical with that of luxurious living, and as such it is mentioned by Anacreon. The iambic poet Semonides of Amorgos disliked smelling perfume and smearing baccharis, and Aristophanes could not stand the stench of the unloosed clothesbag reeking of perfume and ointment. Yet the influence of Sardis was felt in many cities.

Phylarchus, a historian of the third century B.C., records that the people of Colophon, who in the beginning had been rigid in their discipline, later drifted into luxurious habits and became friends with the Lydians. Like them, they went about with long hair adorned with golden ornaments. Xenophanes, too, asserts that the Colophonians learned useless refinements from the Lydians. No less than one thousand of them used to walk to the assembly clad in purple robes, delighted by their beautiful hair, and drenched with the smell of carefully prepared ointments. They became so dissolute that some of them never saw the sun, for fear their skin might not appear as white as possible.

Clearchus of Soli reports that the Sardians set out parks, making them rather like gardens, and in this way lived in the shade, thinking it more luxurious not to have the rays of the sun fall on their skins at all, a practice which we have seen the Colophonians were anxious to follow.

Herodotus tells us that the greatest portion of the work on the mound of Alyattes was performed by the prostitutes. He further informs us that it was the custom for the daughters of the common people of the Sardians to ply this trade to win a dowry for themselves. Xanthus says that the Lydians went so far in wanton luxury that they were the first to sterilize their women, and that the early kings of Lydia employed them in the palace in place of eunuchs.

They went further than this though, and gathered together the wives and maiden daughters of other men into a certain place, which they called, in insolence, the Place of Chastity. There they would use them as they wished. The enormity of this offense was increased because they devised the name for this place from the agnus castus, the tree sacred to Hera, the goddess of marriage, and to Artemis, the peculiar goddess of women. Ultimately, so a legend records, the Lydian men became so completely effeminate that they adopted women's ways of living and, thence, a woman as their tyrant. She was one of those who had been outraged in the Place of Chastity. Being also a woman of unbridled passions, and avenging herself for the indecencies done her, she gave in marriage the daughters of the slave masters to the slaves and, at that, in the very place where she herself had been violated. The Lydians, attempting to shield their embarrassment and her malignity by a euphemism, called the place the Sweet Embrace. The story is too impossible, but it does record an impression of the kind of depths of depravity to which some of their neighbors thought the Sardians sank.

Some say that Polycrates, sixth-century tyrant of Samos, came to his destruction because of the dissipated life he led, emulating the effeminate practices of the Sardians. In fact, Polycrates' demise was engineered by Oroetes, the Persian satrap of Sardis, who lured him to the mainland some twenty years after the death of Croesus, captured, and crucified him. Yet in Samos, Polycrates too built a quarter to rival the park of the Sweet Embrace at Sardis, and in competition with the flowers of Lydia he wove the widely acknowledged "Flowers" of the Samians. He filled Greece with all kinds of exotic foods, tempting to incontinence and sensuality; though by "Flowers" of the Samians, Polycrates is said to have meant the varied charms of women and men, a strangely metaphysical notion.

The people of Sardis were also noted for their dexterity at other kinds of play, at gambling, at dice and knuckle-bones, and even at ball. Living in apparently rather cramped and architecturally uninspired houses, they contrived to live lives of leisure and sensual delight. They titillated their palates for food and sex in devious ways, urged on by the insistent notes of the Lydian lyre; they reaped to the full the rewards of Sardian citizenship and the Mermnad might.

They spoke a language that we do not fully understand (indeed many languages may have been spoken in Mermnad Sardis); they honored their kings with massive funeral mounds after death. They admired the works of the court architects and sculptors and wondered at the press of for-eign dignitaries visiting the golden city. Worshipping their ancestral gods, Cybele, Artemis, and Bacchus, they wit-nessed perhaps the suddenest and briefest cultural explosion in the history of Western man. For one hundred years Sardis was the envy of the world. The visual arts achieved heights hitherto unscaled; riches were the norm and not the exception. In the first half of the sixth century B.C. especial-ly, Sardis shone like a fiery beacon, blazing too brightly amid the other lights of the Western world, signaling her glory and attracting men of genius to her side. Cyrus the Mede snuffed out that beacon with a single devastating stroke, but not before Greek men of discernment had felt its power and learned from the Lydian achievement.

Of Sardis her citizens had been proud.

Selected Bibliography

•

Åkerström, Åke. *Die Architektonischen Terrakotten Kleinasiens.* Lund, 1966.

Akurgal, Ekrem. *Die Kunst Anatoliens von Homer bis Alexander.* Berlin, 1961.

Barnett, R. D. "Early Greek and Oriental Ivories," *Journal of Hellenic Studies,* Vol. LXVIII (1948), 1–25.

Birmingham, J. M. "The Overland Route Across Anatolia in the Eighth and Seventh Centuries B.C.," *Anatolian Studies,* Vol. XI (1961), 185–95.

Bittel, Kurt. *Kleinasiatische Studien.* Istanbul, 1942.

——. *Grundzüge der Vor- und Frühgeschichte Kleinasiens.* 2nd ed. Tübingen, 1950.

Buckler, W. H. *Lydian Inscriptions,* Part II of *Sardis.* Vol. VI, Publications of the American Society for the Excavation of Sardis. Leyden, 1924.

Butler, H. C. *The Excavations,* Part I of *Sardis.* Vol. I, Publications of the American Society for the Excavation of Sardis. Leyden, 1922.

Carruba, O. "Lydisch und Hethitisch," *Zeitschrift der deutschen Morgenlandischen Gesellschaft,* Vol. CXI (1961), 458–63.

Choisy, A. "Note sur les tombeaux lydiens de Sardes," *Revue Archéologique,* Vol. XXXII (1876), 73–81.

Curtis, C. D. *Jewelry and Gold Work,* Part I of *Sardis.* Vol. XIII, Publications of the American Society for the Excavation of Sardis. Rome, 1925.

Dussaud, René. *La Lydie et ses Voisins aux Hautes Époques.* Paris, 1930.

Gelzer, H. "Das Zeitalter des Gyges," *Rheinisches Museum für Philologie,* Vol. XXX (1875), 230–68.

Greifenhagen, A. "Schmuck und Gerät eines lydischen Mädchens," *Antike Kunst,* Vol. VIII, Part I (1965), 13–19.

Gusmani, Roberto. "Neue Inschriften aus Lydien," *Indogermanische Forschungen,* Vol. LXIX (1964), 134–38.

——. *Lydisches Wörterbuch.* Heidelberg, 1964.

Gruben, Gottfried, and Helmut Berve. *Greek Temples, Theatres and Shrines.* New York, 1962.

Hanfmann, G. M. A. *Bulletins of the American Schools of Oriental Research.*

No. 162, "The Third Campaign at Sardis" (1961), 8–49.

No. 166, "The Fourth Campaign at Sardis" (1962), 1–57.

No. 170, "The Fifth Campaign at Sardis" (1963), 1–65.

No. 174, "The Sixth Campaign at Sardis" (1964), 1–58.

No. 177, "The Seventh Campaign at Sardis" (1965), 2–37.

No. 182, "The Eighth Campaign at Sardis" (1966), 2–54.

——. "Horsemen from Sardis," *American Journal of Archaeology,* Vol. XLIX (1945), 570–81.

——. "Lydiaka," *Harvard Studies in Classical Philology,* Vol. LXIII (1958), 65–88.

——. "Prehistoric Sardis," *Studies Presented to David M. Robinson,* Vol. I (St. Louis, 1951), 160–83.

——. "Sardis und Lydien," *Abhandlungen der Akademie der Wissenschaften und Literatur in Mainz,* Geistes- und Sozialwissenschaftlichen Klasse, No. 6 (1960), 497–536.

Hartmann, L. G. "The Date of the Kimmerian Threat Against Assurbanipal According to ABL 1391," *Journal of Near Eastern Studies,* Vol. XXI (1962), 25–37.

Huxley, G. L. *Achaeans and Hittites.* Oxford, 1960.

——. *The Early Ionians.* New York, 1966.

Jacobsthal, P. "The Date of the Ephesian Foundation-Deposit," *Journal of Hellenic Studies*, Vol. LXXI (1951), 85–95.

Kaletsch, H. "Zur Lydischen Chronologie," *Historia*, Vol. VII (1958), 1–47.

Luckenbill, D. D. *Ancient Records of Assyria and Babylonia.* 2 vols. Chicago, 1927.

Masson, O. *Les Fragments du Poète Hipponax.* Paris, 1962.

Miller, M. "The Herodotean Croesus," *Klio*, Vol. XLI (1963), 58–94.

Naster, Paul. *L'Asie Mineure et l'Assyrie aux VIIIᵉ et VIIᵉ siècles av. J.-C.* Louvain, 1938.

Piepkorn, A. C. *Historical Prism Inscriptions of Assurbanipal.* Chicago, 1933.

Radet, G. A. *La Lydie et le monde Grec au temps des Mermnades.* Paris, 1893.

Robert, L. *Nouvelles Inscriptions de Sardes.* Paris, 1964.

Robinson, E. S. G. "Coins from the Ephesian Artemision Reconsidered," *Journal of Hellenic Studies*, Vol. LXXI (1951), 156–67.

Roebuck, C. A. *Ionian Trade and Colonization.* New York, 1959.

Sakellariou, M. B. *La Migration Grecque en Ionie.* Athens, 1958.

Sayce, A. H. "Notes from Journeys in the Troad and Lydia," *Journal of Hellenic Studies*, Vol. I (1880), 87ff.

Shear, T. L. "Sixth Preliminary Report on the American Excavations at Sardis in Asia Minor," *American Journal of Archaeology*, Vol. XXVI (1922), 389–409.

——. *Architectural Terra-Cottas*, Part I of *Sardis*. Vol. X, Publications of the American Society for the Excavation of Sardis. Cambridge, 1926.

Six, J. P. "Monnaies grecques inédites et incertaines," *Numismatic Chronicle* (1890), 202ff.

Smith, Sydney. *Babylonian Historical Texts*. London, 1924.

Thompson, M. "Some Noteworthy Greek Accessions," *Museum Notes* (The American Numismatic Society), Vol. XII (1966), 1–4.

von Olfers, J. F. M. "Über die Lydischen Königsgräber bei Sardes und den Grabhügel des Alyattes," *Abhandlungen der Königlichen Akademie der Wissenschaft in Berlin*, Phil.-Hist. Klasse, (1858 [1859]), 539–56.

Index

◆

143